"I can't think of a more important book that's been written about British wildlife in the past 20 years ... Roy Dennis [is] the UK's pre-eminent conservationist of the past half century ... he writes with such conviction, clarity, insight, depth and purpose. He understands better than anyone how times have changed ... In just a sentence or two, he cuts to the quick ... If you read any book about the environment this year, read this."

JAMES FAIR, Best Nature Books of 2020 in BBC *Countryfile*

"In an exhilarating roundelay of profoundly questioning essays, Roy Dennis has revealed a lifetime in nature conservation, while also delivering a sparkling vision for an ecologically sustainable Highlands, the country and the planet ... [A] testament to a rare and redeeming curiosity; we must all learn from the deep wisdom of experience."

SIR JOHN LISTER-KAYE OBE

"A cracking book full of beautifully descriptive prose and thought-provoking sentiments by a man who, more than anyone else, has been there, done that and got the T-shirt."

IOLO WILLIAMS

"Roy is not just a brilliant conservationist but a superb naturalist too ... These beautiful essays are also positive and pragmatic about the future ... absolutely joyous."

CHRIS PACKHAM

"The wonderful, insightful and eclectic musings from a lifetime watching wildlife, by one of Britain's greatest conservationists."

MIKE DILGER

"Reminds me strongly of Aldo Leopold's *A Sand County Almanac*, which is a classic of the ecological literature, and I can think of no better comparison to give you an idea of its content and of this book's quality and worth ... It is a book of ideas; ideas about how the future should be, but rooted in the present and with knowledge of the past."

MARK AVERY

# Cottongrass Summer

## Essays of a Naturalist throughout the Year

# Roy Dennis

*Saraband*

Published by Saraband
Digital World Centre, 1 Lowry Plaza,
The Quays, Salford, M50 3UB

ISBN: 9781912235889
ebook: 9781912235896

Printed and bound in Great Britain by Clays Ltd, Elcograf S.p.A.

3 4 5 6 7 8 9 10

*Dedicated to all young champions of planet Earth*

# Contents

## Autumn

## Winter

# Introduction

As a child growing up in the Hampshire countryside, I had a very broad interest in nature. One moment I might be climbing a slender tree in a thicket to take a beautifully patterned egg from a jay's nest, the next I'd be hunting under sheets of tin for slow worms or splashing with my gang through a marl pit, catching newts. By my late teens, my interests were focussing more on birds, but even then, when wild camping in the New Forest, a gorgeous pink gladiolus was just as likely to catch my eye as, say, a red-backed shrike.

But birds did win in the end, and I cut my teeth on Lundy Island as a young bird warden. By the age of eighteen, I was an assistant at the famous Fair Isle Bird Observatory. Our day-to-day work revolved around migrations, rare finds and hundreds of thousands of seabirds, and I was fascinated by how these strands were knitted together on this tiny isle, battered by changing weather and towering waves. It made me eager to know more.

A year later, I was working at Loch Garten in the Scottish Highlands, helping to protect Britain's only pair of breeding ospreys. It was a great place to meet people from all walks of life, many of them famous ornithologists who broadened my mind and expanded my knowledge. I remember my first meeting with Doug Weir – later a great friend – when he returned from Alaska with his beautiful sketches of North American wildlife. He told me of the great salmon runs on the Kuskokwim River: about their incredible return from the oceans to spawn in the rivers, thus returning biomass to the land, providing food for wildlife from grizzlies to bald eagles, and enabling ecological renewal throughout the whole ecosystem. This was one of the triggers that encouraged me on my lifelong quest to understand and help nature.

Fighting for wildlife has often made life stressful. Working with the RSPB in the Scottish Highlands in the 1970s and '80s, I was plunged into battle after battle to save a special place or a rare bird. These were years of dramatic change in agriculture, forestry and industry. People often didn't like a relatively young 'birdwatcher' challenging their proposals. I suppose it helped our campaigns for nature that I was good at radio and TV interviews, and at helping journalists understand the issues, but this did not endear me to some developers and politicians. Whatever the stresses, though, fighting for wildlife was never *just* important: it was fun, too.

Later on, one of my friends on the board of Scottish Natural Heritage (SNH) was Bill Ritchie, a lawyer and crofter in Sutherland. While on field trips, we would often have the most esoteric discussions. More practically, he was the first person I knew to use email, and I quickly followed his lead. By then, I was in my mid-fifties and I asked him why he thought I was still prepared to stand up and fight for nature, when friends of my age had decided to lead calmer lives. I explained to him that it was as if I had no choice; that nature was inside me, telling me to do something about the problems it was facing. He said he could understand that feeling and suggested that somehow, because the natural world was under such pressure, it – whatever 'it' was – was persuading more people to take up its cause. I would love to think that was true.

Decades later, I still feel the same way and my life is richer because I continue to champion the natural world. These fifty-two essays – broadly clustered to reflect the changing seasons of nature's year – consider both the problems and progress in ecology and nature conservation. Some have featured in my blogs and other writings. I see this book as a call to thought and action, especially by the young, a book to pick up and dip into, to broaden debate and open minds. Remember that the most important stakeholders (to use today's jargon) are wildlife and the wild places you cherish. Never give up on trying to conserve and restore them. It's essential to try and to succeed; and remember it's never 'if', it's 'when' – and that 'when', ideally, is now.

Good luck.

*Roy Dennis*

# Spring

# Cottongrass

I first found out why cottongrass is special when I went to live near Loch Garten in the Scottish Highlands in April 1960. *Eriophorum angustifolium* is known locally as moss-crop or bog cotton, and of course I'd seen its showy white heads growing in wet areas long before I understood its importance to country life in northern Scotland. It was a friend who told me about it first, because his flock of hoggs – young female blackface sheep – had suddenly started to wander far into the wettest parts of his common grazing in a quest to find it and eat the first signs of spring growth, poking through the ground.

Each spring brought with it the worry that his young sheep would get stuck in boggy patches and drown while on their eager search. It was tough work to pull a sodden sheep safely from a pool full of sphagnum moss. It was worse, of course, if the sheep was already dead.

Appearances deceive. Just as the bog may look safe to walk on yet is treacherous underfoot, moss-crop itself first appears as a tiny, greyish spike but, if pulled gently, reveals three or four inches of bright green, grassy stem. This is what the sheep are after: their first bite of freshness. They are desperate to eat it, even though I was told by old shepherds that it was not, in fact, particularly nutritious. After a cold, hard winter, though, it must taste good.

When I first lived in the Highlands, thousands of hoggs were traditionally taken by lorry from the big sheep farms of the West Highlands to spend their winters on small farms and crofts with common grazings in the central Highlands. It was a way for those farmers to send their future breeding sheep to better grazing for their first winter and to keep them away from the rams at home.

Every late afternoon the flock was let out onto the common graz-ings and then, every morning, the sheep were brought back to the crofts, each of them counted as they dashed through the field gate. The monetary arrangements between the owner of the sheep and the wintering shepherd were often many decades old, and this movement of flocks was a real feature of sheep husbandry in the uplands. Nowadays, it's all but gone.

Interestingly, a few days before my lesson on the importance of cottongrass, I had walked out across the local moor to a blackcock lek. It was daytime, at a spot where the male black grouse were already strutting their stuff at dawn and dusk on the traditional display grounds. I had noted large, fluffy droppings, softer and quite unlike the usual droppings of the grouse family, a mixture of grey and yellow and a bit like dried mousse. Now I understood that the black grouse had been feeding on the shoots of cotton-grass, resulting in the distinctive droppings. Over the following days I noted, using the same observation, that capercaillie and red grouse were also very partial to eating this plant in the early spring, when the frost was leaving the ground.

It is also irresistible to other grazing animals. Suddenly the red deer, which have been grazing in the valley bottoms through the long winter, seem to vanish overnight as they disappear up onto the moors to eat the moss-crop. They have it firmly in their cal-endar of seasonal foods and there's no doubt that the older hinds teach their calves the importance of heading to the hills and bogs to eat the first green spikes of early spring.

Later in the summer, the downy heads of the plant – like fluffy balls of cotton – blow gently in the wind across the wetter moors and bogs, and sometimes catch the sunlight in a most delightful way. I've often stood at the edge of the forest, looking out over the wet peat mosses, and admired the early morning or a low evening sun highlighting this beautiful sedge. I remember a pair of curlews nesting in my favourite moss-crop bog, adding their evocative sound to an already beautiful scene.

I later realised that the snow-white bloom of summer could be an indicator of how many animals were grazing on the land. Early one summer, I was driving along the road over the Struie to Sutherland when my eye caught what I thought were patches of snow on a hill overlooking Edderton. I knew it was too late for snow, but it was enough to make me stop and look with my binoculars across the valley, seeing an amazingly dense hillside of cottongrass heads. Clearly the Forestry Commission stalkers had reduced the deer pressure on that particular part of the forest, and the cottongrass spikes had been allowed to bloom.

Now that there are real efforts – and an urgent need – to encourage natural regeneration by reducing deer numbers, the areas showing a strong growth of cottongrass in the spring are increasing. Too many deer or sheep mean that flowering plants are scarce, so an abundance of cottongrass in bloom in boggy areas is a real marker of successful ecological recovery. For me, it's the perfect mix of beauty and utility, showing us what we're doing right in the simplest and prettiest way.

# All in a name

One spring, we were in a remote mountain valley in the Swiss Alps, the snowy track just opened for the summer. A golden eagle had drifted over the highest belt of trees and we watched a stalking fox pounce on a rodent. Then I saw a great arrow-shaped raptor glide across the lower slopes, soon joined by its mate, their pale heads bright against the dark spruces. '*Lammergeiers!*' I shouted to my Swiss friends. 'Bearded vultures!' came back their reply. They soared back over the great crags of ice and rock and I was reminded that '*lammergeier*' was an old name and in German meant 'lamb killer', a complete misnomer for this great vulture, with its amazing ability to harness marrow from animal bones by dropping them on rocks, the final act in the business of scavenging dead mammals. Miscalling it a lamb killer would not help the recovery of this rare bird in the Alps. Clearly it matters to get the name right.

Older ornithologists like me have seen bird names change – sensibly, hedge sparrow to dunnock, for example – and have had to weather the politically correct renaming of the 1990s, when robins and blackbirds became Eurasian robins and common blackbirds, despite perfectly good scientific names common to birders in every country.

Yet there are times when names are clearly a hindrance to a species, or simply inappropriate. Killer whales enjoy a much better image when called orcas, although the name means much the same thing. And personally, I object to the name 'Minke whale'. When I see one of these wonderful mammals in the seas around the Scottish coasts, I prefer to use 'lesser rorqual' than commemorate the name of a long-gone Norwegian whaler. I'd love to see

'Minke' excised from our books and references. Of course, others might question whether or not it really matters, but consider the public attitude to rats, and then think of another common rodent, the red squirrel. As someone once said, the red squirrel is just a rodent with great PR!

Here in Scotland, though, there is one species that, in my opinion, definitely needs a name change. It is our rarest mammal and in serious trouble: the wildcat. Or is it wild cat (with the space between the two words)? What does wildcat – or wild cat – mean? Does it live in wild places? Not always. Is it wild in the dangerous way? No, never. Is it wild in the untameable sense, as opposed to the tame domestic cat? It is, in fact, a complete misnomer that causes problems for its conservation when one tries to explain to ordinary folk the differences between domestic cats, feral cats (domestic cats living away from houses) or wildcats.

In French, this cat is sometimes called *le chat du bois*, and its scientific species name, *sylvestris*, refers to woods. There's an old English name of 'wood cat' in the history books and scientifically our subspecies is in one of three types, the forest wildcat. It's no help calling it the Scottish wildcat because the species used to live throughout mainland Britain, and could do again in many places. Personally, I also like the sound of a name to commemorate the beautiful diagnostic black rings on its bushy tail – such as 'ring-tailed cat' or 'bar-tailed cat' – but ring-tailed cat is used in North America for a species of raccoon.

Should we have a debate and choose a much more appropriate name? At the time of change, some will say it's nonsense, but give it ten years and the 'new' name would become standard and could be so much better for the future conservation of Britain's 'rarest mammal', *Felis sylvestris*. I think we should reclaim and use the evocative and correct name, the wood cat.

# The optimism of spring

It was one of those gorgeous, early spring-like days of late February in the Scottish Highlands. After early morning frost, the land was sparkling under a bright blue sky and the patches of lying snow gave Strathspey the look of Lapland. With a temperature of 10°C and a fresh westerly wind scudding cotton-wool clouds across the sky, it was a joy to be in the field.

My route took me near a traditional but long-deserted peregrine eyrie where suddenly I saw a shadow high in the sky to the south. A male peregrine falcon was throwing himself up and down in the strong winds, maybe 150 metres above the ancestral nesting cliff. His forebears would have returned here on good days in February every year back through more than five millennia, freshly returned from their lowland wintering quarters to join their mates.

He plunged to the north behind the heather hill and then flashed across the front of the crag. He braked and I thought he was going to land on the ledge where they used to nest. But no, a slight hesitation, and he threw himself upwards, gained height rapidly and, without a backward glance, headed west high over my head. His brief visit had shown him there was no waiting female, no empty scrape nor any distinctive white roosting ledges. The crag was abandoned.

I first visited this nest site in 1960 and soon after reported to a Nature Conservancy scientist that the clutch of eggs had cracked and were leaking. Later, I collected them for him to carry out chemical analysis. This was the lowest point in the peregrine's fortunes, when pesticides destroyed so many eggs and birds. But it was the peregrines of the Highlands of Scotland, living in the most unpolluted part of our islands, which were the bedrock of the recolonisation once the worst chemicals had been banned.

Nowadays, the species is doing incredibly well in towns and cities but is faring disastrously in the once-safe areas that I remember so well in the central and eastern Highlands of Scotland. Most of the eyries on heather moors are empty as a result of continuing illegal persecution on grouse moors. To add insult to injury, many of the peregrine eyries I knew when I was younger, in the north and west of the Highlands, are also abandoned, due to a lack of wild prey: the result of long-term overgrazing and degradation of the land by sheep and red deer.

Today's male peregrine, dancing in the spring skies, was a joy to see. But, alas, it does not yet know that it will have to visit many empty eyries to find a mate, and its chances of being killed before doing so are alarmingly high. In the last ten years I satellite-tagged seven young peregrines in and around the Cairngorms National Park; all of them finally settled in grouse moor areas. In spring, some made day-trip circuits of well over a hundred miles visiting many empty eyries; in the end, none of them survived to breed. Another statistic to add to the appalling illegal onslaught meted out these days to peregrines, golden eagles and hen harriers. Not the sort of pessimism one should feel on such a gorgeous February day in one of the most beautiful parts of our planet, but it's a pessimism that's impossible to ignore.

# Capercaillies and crofters' cows

Sixty years ago, the capercaillie was common in the Scottish conifer forests and its distribution stretched from Sutherland to Argyll. The birds were, in fact, regarded as a pest by foresters because they ate the leading shoots of growing Scots pine trees and could have a real impact on the freshly planted trees from the nursery. They were not so keen on naturally regenerated Scots pine but that's probably because the ones from the nursery had more sugar in them.

I remember capers as plentiful in the conifer woods of the Highlands when I first moved to live in Strathspey in 1960. Some of the display leks at that time could hold more than twenty males. My diary for 16th April 1961 recalls me watching at least fifteen male capercaillies at a dawn lek in Abernethy Forest, with about twenty females in the granny Scots pines or on the ground.

In those years, the capercaillies came out of the woods in autumn to eat grain when the oat stooks were in the fields on small farms and crofts close to the forests. Numbers were so high that estates carried out annual drives to shoot capercaillies and roe deer. Forestry workers in the woods were encouraged to tread on clutches of eggs they came across, and at least one keeper told me that they shot the big young when they were eating wild raspberries growing in the woods. Yet the capercaillies thrived in the vastly increased areas of land planted with Scots pine after the Second World War. It was a real turnaround for a species that became extinct in Scotland in 1785 and was reintroduced from Sweden after a gap of about fifty years.

But by the late 1970s it was clear that the capercaillie was not faring well despite a Scottish population of around 20,000. Non-native Sitka spruce trees were often being planted instead of Scots pine, small farms and crofts stopped stooking oats, predatory mammals such as fox, pine marten and badger increased, and the days of long, hot summers and plentiful insects, important for caper chicks, seemed to drift away into our memories. And so the bird started to disappear from the outlying forests. In the early 1980s, the Forest Commission's Tony Hinde and I conducted a survey of forest rangers in northern Scotland, and that revealed worrying results. Seemingly without many people noticing, capers were absent from many woods and numbers had dropped.

Since those days huge amounts of research have been carried out on the capercaillie, but they are still declining. Special projects such as the wide-scale marking of forest fences to try to prevent collisions have been carried out; there have been working parties, experiments and special funds for management, as well as censuses. In the winter of 2009–10, the survey gave a total of 1,285 capercaillies, while six years later the winter count was 1,114, with 83 per cent of the population now residing in Strathspey. I must say, from my visits to the Strathspey forests, that the latter figure is a very optimistic count for mid-winter. Deterioration in spring and summer weather, especially heavier rainfall, was identified as one of the causes of low chick production. Others blamed losses on an increase in mammal predators.

In my view, the concentration of the species in Strathspey is particularly worrying because of the ever-increasing numbers of people attracted to the Cairngorms National Park, causing disturbance. It's well over ten years now since I wrote to the National Park suggesting the creation of sanctuary areas within the main woodlands that are out of bounds to people during the core breeding season. Additionally, I recommended that dogs be excluded from woodland specially declared for the conservation of capercaillies, whether or not they were on a lead. It's standard practice for nature reserves and national parks in some other countries.

In our ever-changing world, new pastimes appear which do not favour wildlife. I would suggest that night-time mountain biking through capercaillie woodlands and the cutting of bike tracks is inappropriate. There is no doubt that if we want to stop the capercaillie going extinct again – and it would seem extraordinary, in an era of conservation and protection, for that to happen – we have to make some decisive changes within the most important caper forests. If we lose it again, it would be a national disgrace.

The last chunk of old Caledonian Forest was cut down in the 1980s and since then there has been great progress in restoring and expanding native woodlands by the Forestry Commission, private landowners, SNH and the RSPB. A major requirement was to reduce red deer and roe deer to allow natural regeneration, and in many places this has been most successful. But natural management often leads us to a new place, and for several decades I worried that the removal of the deer will be followed by excessive growth of heather, with a thick ground layer of moss in the old pinewoods and the loss of animal tracks. And that's what has happened. We then have to look at how these ecosystems worked in the past. The most important mammal would have been the original wild cattle, the aurochs, which lived in these forests several millennia ago. Their broad grazing behaviour, quite unlike the selective browsing by deer, created glades and multi-ecotones, as well as networks of wide cattle tracks ideal for capercaillies. Most importantly, it allowed the hens to lead the broods of chicks from one good feeding place to another along safe highways. Now it is near enough impossible for them to stumble through metre-high heather. Our ancestors exterminated the aurochs, but their hardy cattle continued to replicate their activities, in some cases through to the middle of the last century. Now regulations and practice have removed cattle from the woods.

When I struggle through the heather jungle in many native pinewoods I feel sorry for female capers trying to rear a family nowadays. Sadly, traditional cattle – what I would call 'crofters' cows' – are now greatly reduced since I first visited the caper woods. In fact, they have probably declined as much as the capercaillie. I don't believe that we will restore the capercaillie in a big way unless we replicate aurochs grazing in the woods. It will require a lot of cattle managed in a low intensive way without any chemical treatments, and in the big forests it will require hundreds rather than tens of animals. I don't think there's time for more research. Just let the staff on the ground get on with innovative management now or it will be too late.

# The beauty of birdsong

One cold spring day, I walked in the early morning up the track from my house to the forest, the sun rising over the larch wood. The birch leaves had just come out and started to cover the trees. They are the most beautiful, gentle shade of green, the sort that makes my heart glad. Whenever I see that colour in spring I think of one of my good friends whom I met one day, many springs ago, on a road above the River Findhorn. We stopped to chat as he was heading to the river to fish for salmon. 'It's time to fish,' he said. 'The birch leaves are as big as a mouse's lug.' It was the sure sign that the salmon would have reached the part of the river where he liked to fish.

As I walked on through the forest, the birch trees' leaves were bigger than a mouse's ear and rang with the song of willow warblers recently returned from Africa. These tiny birds put such energy into letting us all know they are back home. There was a blackcap singing melodiously in the bird cherries – as usual, so well hidden in the foliage – while in clear view at the very top of a tall larch, a song thrush serenaded other thrushes with its beautiful song.

Of course, the spring songs have serious intent as well as beauty. Further on, a wet marshy field held several lapwings displaying with their delightful calls and crazy flying. What an icon of spring that display is, showing other lapwings that this is their bit of Scotland. Here is where their mates will lay four remarkably patterned eggs and hope to rear young. In the spruce wood, a chaffinch was tuning up and informing other chaffinches that that territory was taken.

I love to hear birds in spring song, but that delight is starting to slip away as age eats into my hearing. A hearing aid is never quite the same. How different it used to be when I was able to identify every single bird species that lived in Britain and I could easily hear the really high-pitched ones, like goldcrest, and tricky ones, like grasshopper warbler. Most of my bird recording, especially in woodland, was done by ear rather than by eye, and especially so when I was doing surveys to record the bird species in particular habitats and places.

I learnt the voice of each member of that choir over many years, from the time when I was a child. I wonder now, what was the first song I heard? Blackbird, thrush or woodpigeon? Or was it the purring of turtle doves in the tall garden hedge, where my mother would park me in my pram for my daily fresh air, no matter what the weather? I think it's very difficult to learn birdsong from tape recordings when there are no visual signals of place, time of year or time of day. It's best done as a process, building a memory bank of sound, learning new calls as your experience grows.

By the time I was twelve, I knew the calls and songs of all the common birds living in southern Hampshire. It was this background of aural knowledge that allowed me to add the calls of new species throughout my life as a birdwatcher. Sometimes, though, I was caught out, as on my first walk through the ancient Scots pine trees in the Caledonian forest of Strathspey. I learnt that day the lovely, rippling calls of crested tits, but didn't get the first chaffinches, which in Scotland had a different dialect to the ones I knew in southern England.

There's no doubt that to learn the calls of birds, to enjoy and understand them, is one of the special things about being a birder. Some of them will always stand out in my memory: the high-pitched 'pee-pee-pee' of a displaying male osprey roller-coasting high in the sky in April; the beautiful yodelling of greenshanks flighting over the wet moors of northern Scotland in the evening light; the night-time song of nightingales in thickets when I was very young; and the weird whiplash calls of spotted crakes in a marsh. I'm glad I heard them when I was younger.

Now I will never again hear many of those calls in the wild, some because of my failing hearing, but others because they are no longer there to hear. The creaking of grey partridges, for example, once so common on farms and crofts when the families broke up in March and April, and now so scarce.

So now I listen to the calls I can still hear and look for the others in my memories. When I visit a particular forest, marsh or mountain, there is still a marvellous retrieval from my mind of the beautiful sounds I once heard in those very places. Make sure you listen while your hearing is still sharp, and store those sounds away for safekeeping.

# Too many badgers

When I was a boy in rural Hampshire, badgers were rare and rarely seen. Our Scout troop had a badger-watching setup: the Scoutmaster had scrounged some ancient tractor seats, the ones studded with holes, and these had been carefully hung by ropes in a tree high above a badgers' sett dug in a long bank. If the wind was correct – blowing towards us – we would climb the tree and slide down into a seat. And wait and wait and wait. We finally got to know 'our' badgers very well. Our Scoutmaster was in contact with the author Ernest Neal, who in the 1950s was *the* badger expert in the UK.

Moving north to Strathspey in 1960, I found the badger was rare there as well. There was one big sett near Hamish's farm in Tulloch, and I also knew a big sett near Loch Pityoulish, and a third near the River Spey. At that time, badgers were treated like foxes and otters: snared and trapped to protect hens and livestock, killed for fur and even to make sporrans to wear with kilts. Elsewhere, their bristles were used to make the finest shaving brushes. But I never knew any cases of badger baiting (where they were dug out and forced to fight with terriers) – for me, this cruel, despicable pastime was more of a southern practice. As the years went by, this all became unacceptable and also, progressively, illegal.

Over my lifetime, all of the middle-guild predators – badger, fox, otter and pine marten – became more common, although wildcat became scarcer. Badgers particularly visit grass meadows grazed by cattle, where they can find plentiful supplies of earthworms during their night-time travels. Highland straths provided perfect habitat for the species, so, with protected status, numbers started to climb and they colonised new areas. It became much easier to see badgers, and naturalists started to provide dusk-time hides where people could get their first glimpse of a badger. It became very popular, with the badger the emblem of the Wildlife Trusts.

In England, badgers have often been in the news as the conflict between farmers and badgers over bovine tuberculosis (TB) has raged. The badger/cow/TB scenario has never particularly persuaded me because I believe some of the problem could lie in the fact that dairy cows have been pushed too far to produce increasing amounts of milk as cheaply as possible. In northern Scotland, the greatly increased number of badger setts has impacted on the forestry industry, while infrastructure projects have often involved major expense to accommodate badgers. As the population soared, the numbers of badgers killed on roads has increased and often reflects local densities of setts. On the other hand, I am not sure that the amount of money spent on badger amelioration during road and infrastructure projects is always money well spent for nature conservation.

If I look at the badger situation from an ecological perspective then the lack of a top predator – wolf, lynx and bear – in Britain to regulate the numbers of the middle-guild predators is a real problem. High badger numbers have impacts on smaller mammals – for example, the killing of hedgehogs – and on nesting birds, especially waders like woodcock and oystercatcher, and other ground-nesting species, from skylark to capercaillie. High badger numbers also impact on plant bulbs and ground-nesting bees and wasps. The latter is of particular interest to me as badgers probably impact a favourite bird of mine, the honey buzzard, a very specialised raptor which tracks wasps back to their nests and feeds the nutritious grubs to their young. But many of the wasp nests are in the ground and are dug up and predated by badgers.

Artificial feeding, with peanuts, by badger enthusiasts also helps badgers get over times of food shortage, such as dry summers when worms are scarce; that's good for the badgers but prevents a natural check on numbers – and the absence of top predators means that numbers will stay high.

The badger remains specially protected while the fox can be killed. The two other middle-guild predators, otter and pine marten, have also dramatically increased in the last fifty years and now predate rare birds, such as Slavonian grebe, divers and goldeneye, while pine martens have increasingly predated osprey eggs. All of them are occasionally killed when young by golden eagles, but normal natural predation has been removed by the extinction of the large predators. The real challenge, then, for wildlife conservation is how to deal with these changes and the impacts on other parts of our flora and fauna. It's strange that foxes can be killed but not badgers, while some mainland European hunters are permitted to hunt badgers for food. It is a very tricky issue but one that demands informed debate and action.

# Rewilding – ecological restoration

In recent years, 'rewilding' has become a buzzword. The important thing, though, if it is to become more than a slogan, is that it must be at the forefront of nature conservation. The principle behind rewilding is not new, it's just that it's not been taken up, which is why the efforts of George Monbiot and his friends in setting up the charity Rewilding Britain are so important. I've been involved in ecological restoration (another name for rewilding) for much of my working life and it's important to recognise that others have trod the same path, especially Sir Frank Fraser Darling in the 1950s, who drew attention to the degraded 'wet deserts' of Scotland. No one, though, wanted to listen. He went off to work as an ecologist in North America where his wise advice was valued.

The aim of rewilding is to restore nature and natural processes over much larger areas of land, rather than concentrate on small nature reserves. It's also aimed at the whole ecosystem, so it's about functions as well as individual species. It's about restoring soils, vegetation, invertebrates, mammals and birds, as well as capturing carbon, producing oxygen, the natural management of water and local climate. It's truly about life on Earth.

The problem is that it will require major changes in land use, which will not necessarily be welcomed by those with traditional interests on the land. It may often not fit even with some people working in nature conservation. I remember when I worked with the RSPB in the Scottish Highlands in the late 1980s, and we came up with a really big ecological restoration project with the owner of Sutherland Estates. At the very last moment I visited the RSPB headquarters in England to finalise the project, but, out of the blue,

I was told to abandon it because one of the senior managers, a scientist, was worried about any future risks to his scientific credibility. 'I don't want someone examining the project in forty years' time and finding it did not work as expected.' The landowner in Golspie thought we had lost our senses. So did I.

In the 1990s, I first went to the Oostvaardersplassen nature reserve in the Netherlands to see the groundbreaking work pioneered by Frans Vera, Hans Kampf and Fred Baertelman: they released Polish Konik ponies, Heck cattle and red deer in a large area of marshland. The large herbivores thrived over the years and their impacts were very exciting as different species and plants came to the fore during the successions. It was the large scale of the project that allowed these exciting processes to take place, in contrast to small reserves where management plans often say, 'This bird lives here,' and, 'That plant will grow there.' What we need is 'bigness', so that natural processes are the driver rather than the management plan. In Britain, good recent examples are Knepp Estate in Sussex, along with Abernethy Forest and Glenfeshie in the Scottish Highlands, but excitingly there are many places now where ecological restoration comes first. There has to be many more and in much bigger areas.

Concerns over global climate breakdown are making us address new and worrying events, and the severe flooding impacting many people's homes and livelihoods in the recent past has been a real catalyst in making us realise that the management of the land is more important than the building of expensive flood defences alone. This gives a real opportunity for conservation people and organisations to make a concerted effort to get change.

It's going to be really difficult because so many people have entrenched views about how the land should be used. But it's the scale that is important. I used to say that 30 to 40 per cent of our lands and seas should be principally managed for nature and functioning ecosystems. Interestingly, even I'm a bit on the modest side, as Professor Edward Wilson of Harvard University, a real visionary on these issues, says that nature needs half of the Earth. The title of his book – *Half-Earth* – says it all.

So how do we go about it? We need a bigger vision. We cannot have large areas of land in a degraded state – by which I mean the bare, degraded uplands of Britain. We must have larger areas of native woodlands and we have to address intensive large-scale farming and its impacts on the environment. Just because we farmed in this way in the past is not to say that it's in the best interests of society in the future.

We can start by looking at some of our best examples of nature and then making them bigger, doubling or tripling them. I've always thought that special places, like Rutland Water, should be surrounded by flower meadows, marshes and natural woodlands. A buffer zone of a kilometre, where farming is minimal or ceased, would be a start. We have many other places in our land where a nature conservation gem surrounded by modern agriculture could be incredibly enhanced by doubling or tripling its size.

# Cheaper food and poorer farming

There's no doubt that this is a difficult time for farming because we all want cheaper food, and that's what the supermarkets provide. That's not necessarily in the best interests of farming, nor of farmers. Most of Scotland's farms – especially those that are tenanted – have traditionally had a clause in the lease that says 'the farmer is required to keep the land in good heart'. It's understood that the land should be passed on to future generations in as good or better condition. The problem with the race for cheaper and cheaper food is that 'good heart' has been and is being eroded. Soils, instead of being a rich mix of soil invertebrates, worms, humus and fungi, become nothing but a medium for holding artificial fertilisers. It was shocking to hear comments in the 2015 'International Year of Soils' that some soils have only got another hundred harvests in them. That should be a real wake-up call, but I doubt that it will be, even though the worldwide estimated loss of topsoil due to intensive agriculture is 25 to 40 billion tonnes per annum.

Most farmers don't like being told what's good for society, rather than what's good for them, and farmers also know that it's always worth complaining. It's a tried and tested method, along with never saying that you've done well. Farming is also, to them, a matter of common sense that people in towns don't really understand. As someone who helped run a croft with cattle and sheep for fifteen years, I can empathise with that. There's nothing like standing with your stock or the crops you've grown on your farm for making you feel special. It's our ancient genes coming out.

So what should be the future for farming? It must involve better recognition of the long-term duty to keep soils in good heart. In many areas, the system of rotational cropping has been abandoned in the face of economic pressures and the drive for cheaper food. Deep ploughing is also an anathema to the soil fauna. When I look at the area in which I live in Moray, I'm concerned about the loss of soils due to wind erosion in dry springs. I remember in May, a few years ago, driving into my local town of Forres, with the dust storm blotting out the approaches to the town reminiscent of films from the Sahara. Thousands of tons of soil must have been blown out to sea that day; it made me so angry that I wrote to the government minister responsible. His department replied telling me about all the regulations regarding farming and soils, and basically assuring me that there's plenty of soil. I guess they do not know their history: many of the best farmlands of ancient Rome were in North Africa and are now deserts due to overuse.

I also wonder about the ecological impacts of the drive to grow more barley to sustain the ever-increasing export market of Scotch whisky, which saw a 7.8 per cent growth in 2018, to a record £4.7 billion. This may be excellent news for Scotland's balance of payments, for the farmers and, especially, for the distillers. But is there enough thought about the long-term impacts on our soils, as opposed to profits and share prices? There's already been a little talk about a Moray water tax on each bottle of whisky to pay for the use of Scotland's iconic water. I think the whisky drinker, through the whisky industry, should also pay an ecological levy per bottle to help maintain the soils. Meanwhile, the industry continues to eat into the biological capital of farmland, which must be safeguarded for future generations. That's the responsibility of good government.

# The tragedy of rare flowers

One of the delights of a walk up the road from my house in spring is the gorgeous display of cowslips blooming in the grass verge. When I first found it, I was very excited and went straight to Mary McCallum Webster's book, *Flora of Moray, Nairn & East Inverness*. 'Found in some localities, almost certainly escapes,' she wrote. A few years later I was talking to a friend who had lived in the farmhouse at the end of our road. 'Oh, they're mine!' she said excitedly. I asked her what she meant. Long ago, when she lived near Rugby, one of her favourite walks was along a deserted railway line where cowslips bloomed. One year, she told me, she collected lots of seed and when she next came north, she sprinkled it along the roadside, where they grew. Now I knew the history of this small patch of yellow flowers, the only ones I am aware of in this part of the world.

Do flowers need to be rare to be special? It's a tragedy that so many of our flowers now are uncommon, usually as a result of overgrazing by domestic stock, widespread burning and, over the decades, increasing intensification of agriculture and forestry. Many years ago, while at a conference in Cirencester, I made a special trip to look at a field of snakeshead fritillaries near Cricklade. They were absolutely beautiful, but why do they have to be so scarce? I saw lots of cowslips as well, but they were mainly on roadsides rather than the fields. Another time, in Norfolk, I saw in the distance a large field of brilliant yellow. My Natural England colleague explained that it was a mass of cowslips, planted and encouraged by a thoughtful landowner. I remembered, years earlier in the 1990s, when I was on the board of Scottish Natural Heritage, staff would present the latest display and thinking on wild flower conservation, which always seemed to include a no-pick clause. I said that we must therefore make certain that wild flowers are much more plentiful and widely spread in the countryside, so that the old tradition of small children picking a bunch of wild flowers for their mothers can continue.

I've often wondered why we keep rare flowers so rare. Sometimes, as in ornithology, it seems that some botanists like species to be rare, offering something special on their 'patch', a gem to be shared with a botanist friend from another part of the country. They, in turn, might have rare orchids on their home patch, and would be proud to show them in return. There wouldn't be the same kudos if they became commoner.

Occasionally, when I've been in the forests monitoring osprey nests, I've come across the iconic twinflower, with its two tiny pink trumpets on a lowly creeping plant. It's the plant that the famous Swedish botanist Linnaeus named after himself – *Linnaea borealis*. I'm sure its rarity is the result of very long-term woodland overgrazing and forestry practices, including burning. There are other rare gems, such as one-flowered wintergreen and, in the mountains, the alpine blue-sow-thistle. I've always encouraged the idea that we should learn how to propagate these rare flowers and increase their distribution, and I once moved a few patches of twinflower to another pine forest in the hope that they would flourish. My success was limited: only one grew.

Now that we are witnessing some great examples of natural regeneration or planting of native woods, we have to learn how to add the rest of the flora. Why is it acceptable to plant Scots pine, birch or aspen, yet to introduce rare plants seems to be frowned on? We have to learn to think about what else should be in these restored forests and do something about it. I am pleased that tentative steps are being made to make rare plants commoner, but it has to be done more widely and more urgently. We will have succeeded when twinflower and its ilk are no longer rare plants.

It is, of course, a worldwide problem. One recent spring, when I visited my daughter Rona in Crete, her husband Erik took me to some mountain fields of oats where the usually ever-present goats and sheep had been excluded. I had read that the island has three endemic tulips and, one of them, the beautiful red Cretan tulip, had been in flower in these fields when Rona and Erik had visited a few weeks before. Alas, the tulips were over and just one late bloom remained, but I was rewarded by the variety and numbers of orchids and the ever-present singing of corn buntings. Rona and Erik had been shown the tulip field by a Dutch botanist who told them that the species in the wild was restricted to this small field, of less than one acre, and one other smaller one. And that was it. While the locals practice very low-intensive agriculture based on the growing of oats, they should be safe, if precarious. If this way of farming came to an end, though, and goats were allowed in, the flower would be lost. This is clearly another case in which mankind needs to set aside larger areas of nature if it is to maintain the incredible beauty and diversity of planet Earth.

# Nature's networks

It was one of those beautiful spring evenings in the Scottish Highlands. I had worked at home most of the day so was happy to head off to my local patch – Findhorn Bay – on a special search. As I crossed the saltmarsh, recently grazed by thousands of pink-footed geese, I walked through a dense white carpet of scurvy grass flowers; it was like walking through snow, though beautifully scented and warmer underfoot. The first osprey hung in the sky over the bay and a scan with binoculars showed three male ospreys hovering a few hundred feet above the incoming tide. They were finding it hard to spot their prey in the choppy water. Then one of them caught a flounder and set off inland to its mate, waiting on her nest of eggs for the evening meal.

But, for once, I was not here to watch ospreys but to look at one of the spring wonders of Findhorn Bay, on the Moray coast. It's a regular staging post for the spring migration of Arctic ringed plovers, on their way from Africa to the high Arctic. They are always with northern dunlin, so I made my way over to sit on a big tree trunk embedded in the mud. This great tree had been washed down the river in last August's huge flood and was now a favourite perch for ospreys. On the edge of the tide I found a larger flock of waders than I expected – with my telescope I estimated 900 ringed plovers and 600 dunlins, with three summer plumage sanderlings. The sun was behind me, so the birds were in full sunlight. There was a strong and surprisingly cold wind blowing from the north, and I was so glad I had put on my thickest fleece and a woollen hat.

The waders came closer and closer as the tide pushed them towards me; the dunlins were mostly in beautiful summer plumage, with reddish-brown backs and jet-black bellies, and they were as busy as sewing machines, stabbing the mud with their bills catching food.

The Arctic race of the ringed plover is smaller than our local breeding ringed plovers. They were looking gorgeous in their smart black and white stripes, running back and forth and feeding from the surface. But what I really love about these spring gatherings of ringed plovers is their busyness and exuberance. They run at each other and then individuals jump in the air and flick their feathers – a continuous sense of excitement. It's like watching the start of a kids' race at school, everyone eager to get going. These waders want to get to their Greenland breeding grounds, but who within the flock is saying, 'This north wind is too strong and it's cold; we need to wait'? Are the flighty ones youngsters? Or is it that the weather suddenly changes and the whole flock knows that this is now the time to make the next stage of that great migration?

Many summers ago, I camped among these waders breeding in north-east Greenland, and it's still fresh in my memory, seeing them scuttling over stones and moss among the beautiful blossoms of the Arctic flowers. My memory, though, is more vivid when I think of their summer neighbours, musk ox and polar wolves. So when I see ospreys hovering above a flock of Arctic ringed plovers in Findhorn Bay, I think of those iconic white wolves in that far country. And as I sat on my log watching the waders, I knew that a thousand years ago ospreys hunting this same bay would have had every chance of seeing grey wolves in Scotland. I would love that to be a possibility again, and the sooner we restore wildness, the better.

At 9 p.m., I walked back to my car, the golden sun still hanging above Culbin Forest; nature at its very best.

# Bearded vulture and a lack of carrion

In May 2016, Britain's first ever-recorded bearded vulture was seen in the wild, first of all in Gwent and then on Dartmoor. It seemed likely it was the young vulture seen in Belgium on 9th May, and it was thought to be a wild bird from the mainland European population, which is increasing following some excellent recovery conservation.

It must have had a shock coming to our country – a bit like our going to the supermarket to find all the shelves empty – because its natural food is the final remains of large dead mammals. Our farm regulations insist on all dead livestock being cleaned up from the countryside. The bearded vulture is the last species in the chain of vultures that eat large animal carcasses. After the griffons and black vultures have feasted on the carcass, the bearded vulture is the ultimate scavenger, swallowing bones and breaking larger ones by dropping them from a height onto rocks and eating the marrow. Nowadays in our sanitised countryside, generally devoid of dead animals, there's not much opportunity for burying beetles, bone fungi or bearded vultures. A sign of a damaged ecosystem.

In fact, the removal of calcium in the form of bones from the countryside is a major change in recent centuries. This is particularly problematic in the uplands where calcium is scarce, and the annual loss in the form of sheep and cattle bones is massive, as stock goes to market. It must be thousands of tons per year, and nowadays even the bones of most red deer are carried off the hills. But how is this loss of calcium a problem for the ecosystem? I learnt recently that the eggs of the ring ouzel, the mountain blackbird, had become thinner and thus more vulnerable, probably because of losses of calcium in the uplands caused by acid rain.

I'm not suggesting female ring ouzels should eat bones before laying their eggs, but there's no doubt that any bone or deer antler left in the countryside is quickly gnawed by other creatures seeking calcium. It's all part of the web of life in which we live.

In order to reduce the excessive numbers of deer in Scotland and to promote natural regeneration of flora, most conservation bodies are involved in the killing of deer. When challenged about this by people who do not like the idea of deer being killed, conservationists often state that culling is necessary because of the missing predators, such as wolves and lynx, which have been removed from the system. But the important thing about predators is that they do not eat all of the animals they kill. They can leave, quite often, as much meat and carrion *in situ* as they eat. This is then available to a whole range of carrion eaters, from eagles, kites, ravens, foxes and martens down to burying beetles. They also kill throughout the year and they kill randomly throughout their home range.

On most or all nature reserves and protected areas, carcasses are removed from the reserve and sold into the venison market. In some cases, even the grallochs, heads and other remains are buried. We now recognise that the removal of mature trees is no longer acceptable on nature reserves, and that dead trees can be more valuable for wildlife than live ones. I believe that the removal of biomass in the shape of large dead herbivores, such as red deer and roe deer, is similarly damaging to the ecosystem of nature reserves. The elimination of part of the food chain running from the sun's energy to plant production to herbivore to carnivore is damaging, and in many cases – in low-productivity habitats – it is not just the removal of the carrion but also the loss of calcium in the bones of the animals that is very damaging to the system. So the removal of deer carcasses from nature reserves and protected areas should cease, and the use of copper bullets, which are not toxic, instead of lead should be mandatory.

This would in part replicate what it was like when deer were killed and eaten by wolves or died of old age; it would help carrion eaters, and it would fertilise plants and provide hosts for fungi. This may run counter to our fixation on health and cleanliness, but it is important: wild animals have died and been killed within the environment for millions of years and nature is competent at recycling this biomass. It is all part of the natural food chain.

In recent decades, the whole question of leaving dead domestic animals on open land has been the subject of increasing change. There are, of course, some rational concerns about the possible transference of disease – for example, during foot and mouth outbreaks – and also problems with scavenging by dogs. But carcasses have often been an important food source for some of our most distinctive wildlife including, in Scotland, white-tailed and golden eagles.

The importance of carrion for key wildlife species has been recognised in derogations available in France and Spain allowing carcasses to be left out for the feeding of vultures. And within UK legislation, the Animal Health Act included a provision for the use of dead domestic animals for the specific purpose of feeding carrion eaters such as raptors. But in recent years, the combined problems of foot and mouth disease, BSE and new legislation from the European Union have resulted in increasing restrictions on the leaving of dead domestic animals in the open countryside. In fact, it's getting to the stage where this might be completely forbidden.

It is alarming to hear people in authority suggesting that dead animals on open land or in the mountains are either dirty or a danger to the health of humans. Always in my mind in these discussions is my memory of a mere outline of a long-dead musk ox on a hill slope in north-east Greenland that was thronged with yellow poppies, all a benefit from the decayed carcass.

It's interesting where thinking about a lost bearded vulture takes us. I just hope it found a big dead animal in Dartmoor National Park. Perhaps someone could put out a couple of dead horses for the next one to arrive. You never know: it could be the first step in the vulture recolonisation of Britain.

# Storks and people

When I was a boy, one of my favourite locations for birdwatching was St. Catherine's Point, at the southern tip of the Isle of Wight. We used to sit with our backs to the stone wall surrounding the lighthouse, looking out to sea with our binoculars, telescopes and notebooks. It was a brilliant place to observe the visible migration of birds. In spring we watched the hurrying flocks of chestnut-plumaged bar-tailed godwits or common scoters heading east through the English Channel, flocks of pipits coming in off the sea from France and, in autumn, coasting flocks of swallows and martins heading south for the winter.

Much later, in the early years of this century, while working on a successful project to restore breeding ospreys to Andalucía, I got to know the southern coast of Spain at Tarifa. There, the annual migrations of large raptors, especially short-toed eagles, vultures and honey buzzards, are legendary. But I also marvelled at the great flocks of white storks thermalling high into the sky before setting off across the Straits of Gibraltar to Morocco.

These dramatic migrations are such an icon of the exuberance of the arrival of spring or the sadness of the approach of winter. Long, long ago in Britain, the annual migrations of big recognisable birds, like storks and cranes, would have held deep significance for our ancestors. These were the landmarks of their years, rather than being governed by the busyness of present-day work and life. That's why they are remembered in legend, place names and carvings. My friend Lorcan O'Toole wrote a thought-provoking book, *Corr Scéal – Crane Notions*, about the role and meaning of cranes in pre-Christian Ireland. No wonder that in our genes they still hold great significance and that the crying of cranes goes straight to our hearts.

In an era of a monstrous loss of nature, in which it appears impossible to restore on a large scale the common species of my childhood, such as yellowhammer, grey partridge, poppies and water voles, we can achieve real success with some of the bigger species, simply because they mean so much to us. That's why our projects on ospreys, sea eagles and red kites have been so successful, as has been the present work with cranes and beavers: removing human persecution is the key to some problems.

This is also why the project to restore the white stork as a British breeding bird has all the hallmarks of being successful. Since early man, the white stork has been held in esteem in the British Isles as well as in many parts of the world. Just imagine the thrill in the future of seeing flocks of white storks thermalling up into late summer skies to cross the English Channel from the Isle of Wight, Beachy Head or the white cliffs of Dover after their breeding season in Sussex.

Then why not the black stork as well? It's a species whose fortunes have changed in recent decades in Europe. In the 1970s I went to Poland for the first time and visited the fantastic Biebrza Marshes – an incredible area for wildlife. That first view stays with me still, getting out of the coach from the city and looking down from a hill onto marshes dotted with haystacks in the early morning mists and hearing a multitude of corncrakes. There were lots of white storks in the villages but the black stork was, at that time, incredibly rare. Finally, one of our birding guides agreed to show us a black stork's nest if we kept the location secret. We headed off with him into a big, dense forest and finally, after a good hike, came to a huge oak tree. In the fork was a big stick nest with a brood of young black storks, standing up. He told us this was a special nest; it was exactly on the boundary of two communes and the reason he had to keep it secret was that the black stork was still thought of as a harbinger of death – so different from the attitude towards its white cousin, which signified birth and renewal. He said that some older people would still search for the nest of the black stork on their land and destroy it, just in case.

In the years since, times have changed, nature conservationists have persuaded country people in Europe to look more kindly on the black stork, and its numbers have increased. On a repeat visit to Poland in the 1990s I saw a dozen standing in a wet marshy field. I've even seen them in Scotland on a couple of occasions, and in 2017 there was a lovely record of one visiting a beaver marsh. No one saw it, but its image was later found on a trail camera set to record the activities of the beaver family. At several places in Germany and Belgium I have seen this association between beavers and black storks. Now that the beaver is making a gradual return to the British Isles, it would be wonderful to have the black stork restored to our country and living in woodland streams, in the company of beavers, like long ago. People occasionally ask me whether they bred here and I reply that Pliny recorded them in his writings about a visit during the Roman occupation. Remembering the plunder of large water birds long ago, though, and thinking of our European countryside of woods and streams, it's clear that they were here in history and that they should come back.

# Green J is back again

In May 2016, I had a phone call from a friend telling me that an osprey nest on his land, which had not been used for nearly a decade, was being rebuilt by a pair of ospreys. A few days later, I was there with him and we were amazed to identify, with our telescopes, that the female was in fact a twenty-five-year-old bird named Green J. I had ringed her as a chick in Easter Ross in 1991 (her green colour ring inscribed with a capital 'J'), and she had bred at a nest near Carrbridge in Strathspey since 1995. She was an excellent breeder, producing many young, some of which were translocated to Rutland Water and later to Andalucía or, more recently, to the Basque country.

She was the very first osprey in the UK to be fitted with a state-of-the-art satellite transmitter. That was in 1999 and that autumn, when visiting Extremadura in Spain, I found her fishing at a lake, being hassled by the local jackdaws. We then learned that she wintered at Gabriel y Galán reservoir in central Spain and did not migrate to Africa at all. She was almost certainly our most northerly wintering Scottish osprey. The transmitter was removed after a few years, but in 2013 we again caught her near her nest and satellite tracked her, for I wanted to know whether she would ever venture to Africa. After all those years, we again followed her migration south through England and France, then she turned south-west over northern Spain and headed straight to the Gabriel y Galán reservoir in Extremadura.

In the summer of 2015, Green J was unceremoniously kicked out of her nest by a large young female osprey and she also lost her mate. She left Strathspey early and we tracked her wandering up the River Spey past Kingussie and then lost contact with the transmitter. We were worried that she might have died. We were wrong, though, because a Spanish ornithologist friend was sure he saw her that winter at her favourite reservoir. He'd clearly been right: she returned again to Strathspey and, when we monitored the new nest, we could see that she was incubating eggs. She was with a new mate, a young male from southern Scotland, and they went on to rear two young, proving that she was still a capable mother despite her age. I also checked her old nest and found that the previous year's intruder had also found a new mate; they went on to rear a single chick.

Also in May 2016, we visited Red 8T, a male osprey very well known to the bird photographers who regularly visited the Aviemore fisheries; he was circling with an intruding male osprey close to his usual nest, while his regular mate was incubating eggs. Near my home in Moray, an old female, Morven, had also returned for another year; she mated with the same male as the previous year and was incubating eggs in the same nest. She had two late young that were below weight when we went to ring them. One of them I collected under licence for the Swiss osprey reintroduction project, while the other rapidly thrived on his own and was successfully reared.

I've followed the fortunes of these ospreys for nearly sixty years, watching individuals start breeding and disappear; some lasting just one year or a few seasons while others continue into old age, like the veteran female Green J, still breeding at twenty-five years old. It's funny, really: I should accept that I, too, am getting older and can't climb trees like I used to when there were just a few pairs breeding in Scotland. But in the company of ospreys, it's easy to forget.

# Selective land management
# in Abernethy Forest

I lived at the RSPB Osprey Camp at Inchdryne in Tulloch during the spring and summer from 1960 to 1963. After seven years in the Shetlands, I returned to work as the Highland Officer of the RSPB in 1971, and from 1984 to 2005 I lived at and helped work the croft of Inchdryne in Strathspey.

Crofting life in the Scottish Highlands in the early '60s had hardly changed for a century, except with the arrival of the first small, grey Fergie tractors and associated equipment. Each croft in Tulloch had cows, some of which were milked, and cream, butter and cheese were made and consumed on the croft. The croft land was fully utilised to grow hay, oats, potatoes and turnips on a rotation, with some fields, and the outbye and common land, used for grazing. Cattle were kept in the byres in the winter so that each croft had a big dung heap, which was truly essential for spreading on the fields before ploughing in the spring. Chickens, ducks and sometimes geese were kept for eggs and food. Some crofts had quite large numbers of beehives and sold the honey to holidaymakers in summer. Oats were cut in sheaves and stored on the croft in big ricks, which were threshed in the winter by a travelling threshing mill. During the winter, the cows were fed hay in the hecks above their stalls, as well as chopped turnips and bruised oats. They were let out each day to get water from the burn. Generally, the crofts and small farms wintered large numbers of blackface hoggs (young female sheep) from the West Highlands and these were put out onto the common grazings in the late afternoon and brought back in the morning, and then often fed oats in their troughs and chopped neaps, especially during snow. At these times, chaffinches and yellowhammers fed with the sheep in large numbers. Grey partridges, oystercatcher and lapwings nested on the crofts.

Strathspey Estates, which owned the land, were regularly on the ground, with the factor and his staff visiting the crofts. I remember the crofts and farms being very well worked and very open in aspect compared to the present day. There was a very clear distinction between the croft land and what the locals and the estate called 'The Forest'. The latter, with its 'Forest Fence', was out of bounds to stock and also to wood collection and hunting. The estate gamekeepers, based at Forest Lodge, would be seen in The Forest, on the hill ground and across the crofts.

The Head Forester for Abernethy, William Marshall, who lived in Nethybridge, was a good friend, very knowledgeable about wildlife and an old friend to the RSPB. He had quite a staff based at the tree nursery at the Dell, on the edge of Nethybridge, and they were regularly working in The Forest, often in-filling with planted Scots pine in the gaps between natural regeneration, but also harvesting, clearing ditches and so on. Annual drives were held to shoot roe deer and the numerous capercaillie, regarded as pests. Because of the very active land use and the high usage of the croft lands and common grazings by cattle and sheep, scrubland was very minimal; in fact, I think the only real extent of willow scrub in 1960 was in the bogs near Delbog.

As I remember it, the Forest of Abernethy was pure Scots pine in the early 1960s and any odd broadleaf tree such as birch or willow that suddenly popped up would be cut down by one of the woodmen, who went about their business on a bicycle with a bush-saw and a spade. A small birch with fresh green leaves in The Forest was an easily seen target among the pines. The forest bogs near the osprey nest, behind Inchdryne and on Tulloch moor, were very open, with just clumps of Scots pine on the drier hillocks and curlews nesting in the bogs. I was told that Loch Garten and Abernethy Forest were very dear to the Countess of Seafield and her family. They enjoyed seeing the Caledonian Forest as they thought it should be: made up solely of Scots pine.

In retrospect, it is clear to me that there was a very high degree of management favouring Scots pines in The Forest by the removal of scrub and deciduous trees. It is difficult in this mechanised day-and-age to imagine the degree of intimate management both in The Forest and on the crofts and common grazings. Crofters and farmers at that time were very particular about having their ground in 'good heart'; ditches were always cleaned out annually, often by travelling people who pitched up in the same place every early spring, camped somewhere on the croft for a few days and cleaned all the ditches by hand with a spade, for which they received various goods such as milk, butter, potatoes, maybe tobacco and a little cash. This meant that there was no – or very little – boggy ground on crofts and certainly no willow bushes. I was told quite clearly that willow bushes growing on a croft were a sign of a bad crofter (at a time when these views were important).

Suddenly, in the late 1960s and into the 1970s, everything started to change in farming and crofting, and the old traditions were lost surprisingly quickly. What is important now is to recognise that when we look at the 'natural' landscape, human impacts had been leaving their mark for hundreds of years; some maybe on a large scale, such as big forest clearances for timber, and some on a local scale, by each individual crofter or farmer. It is therefore simply not true to say that these lands are untouched by humans and are truly natural.

# Summer

# The decline of swifts and martins

One recent spring, I enjoyed watching swifts *en masse* – not in Scotland but at my daughter's home in Crete. She has an interesting house in the old centre of Chania, among an amazing townscape of ancient houses, buildings and tightly twisting streets. No two houses are alike, so there are lots of crevices under tiles and holes in walls, just perfect for swifts. Sitting out on the roof terrace, three storeys up, the swifts were my ever-present neighbours as I enjoyed the sun and the views. They would whizz at high speed past my lookout, small groups of six or seven engaging in the most madcap flying and screaming all the while. It was magical to watch and I never tired of their exuberance as I read my holiday paperbacks. Goodness knows how many pairs breed in Chania but one morning I estimated 700 in the air at one time over the old part of the town. Then there were their mates in nests and many, many more in the rest of the city.

It reminded me, a little, of the 1960s when screaming parties of swifts would fly up and down the street in Boat of Garten on summer evenings while we were having a nice beer outside the pub. The same was true of most Highland villages and towns, but when I look now over Forres, near my home in Moray, I'm lucky to see half a dozen swifts in the air at one time.

There has, of course, been a massive decline in flying insects since we started using so many chemical sprays for modern agriculture and to sustain our way of life. But renovating old houses is also bad news for swifts – building inspectors hate holes in buildings, so there are no longer cracks under roofs or crannies in walls – while new buildings are even worse. I've seen the old houses in our local villages progressively improved for people but lost to swifts and bats. I remember how difficult it was to convince the workmen renovating a big Highland shooting lodge to leave open the swift and bat entrances under the eaves. Several times I had to scrape out the new mortar to open a route for the swifts to their nests; the owner was keen on wildlife conservation and wanted swifts and bats to thrive.

Swallows are also having a hard time as more and more derelict buildings, barns and sheds are turned into desirable country living quarters. The farmyards are not as mucky as they used to be when farms had cattle and horses, open barns and byres, and a farm pond with muddy edges. Then there were lots of insects and also plentiful mud to make their nests.

Sand martins suffer from other ways in which we tidy up. When I was young there were lots of sand pits in the countryside. Farmers and landowners would open up a sandpit and whenever they needed sand for building, they would go and expose the bank. Many of these sandpits were used by sand martins, sometimes losing their nesting banks but soon finding new, exposed sand. If sandpits are not regularly used, however, the angle of the bank changes from vertical to sloping, allowing the nesting holes to be reached more easily by stoats and pine martens, which predate the nesting martins. Nowadays, opening sandpits means paperwork and then they have to be landscaped after use, which martins hate. Road cuttings were also favoured nesting banks for sand martins but they, too, have to be tidied up now. I remember a big colony above a road near the River Spey before, to my horror, it was landscaped.

An increasing number of concerned people are building 'nest chambers' for swifts and I've seen illustrations of beautiful nesting towers built for them. There are special building blocks, with nesting holes, which can be incorporated into the design and build of new houses, and I hope more and more of these will be used. Sand martins can be encouraged to use purpose-built sand martin walls and they love them, but if only they could access a few more old-style sandpits and old houses with crevices.

And – for our and their sakes – we need to stop the chemical onslaught on the countryside. Spraying is killing our future. Progress does not always take us towards a better world and I, for one, find more drama in watching bands of swifts screaming overhead than I do in watching television.

# Caring for our planet
# – a minister's responsibilities

I remember a radio interview from 2015, when I heard Richard Lochhead MSP, the then Cabinet Secretary for Rural Affairs, being harangued by the fishermen's leader for taking a tough stance on scallop dredging off the Wester Ross coast. The next day, he was being taken to account by the scientific community for the government stand on genetically modified crops. Whenever I hear such trenchant comments, my general reaction is that the politician in question has probably got something right and is treading on the toes of vested interests.

In what, I hope, is a forward-looking Scotland, it's really pertinent to ask who the minister should be standing up for. Too often, political decisions are short-term and politicians can offer all sorts of inducements to change voting patterns. Our future on this Earth is a question of much debate in an era of climate breakdown and biodiversity collapse, so one must ask whether Cabinet Secretaries for Rural Affairs should be mainly looking after the interests of those people active in the areas covered by their department, or whether they should be thinking about society as a whole – about all of Scotland's people, whether they live in the countryside or in the city. And, importantly, I believe that they should have their eye not just on the people of today but also be thinking seriously about their government's responsibilities to those people's grandchildren and their grandchildren's grandchildren. They also need to address Scotland's stance on, and contribution to, the health of planet Earth.

It's a tough job but that should be why people go into politics. And, whatever they say in public, you know that they had been advised by their civil servants who are, in general, likely to tell them to take a careful approach rather than be bold, as at times they should be.

During the run-up to the Scottish referendum and particularly on television programmes with a UK audience, it was very interesting to see our First Minister calling for a much fairer society. It seemed to strike a chord with people throughout the British Isles and must be an important part of the future of Scotland. Nicola Sturgeon's viewpoint has a clear message for how we live in Scotland.

We are all in the same boat, and I'm not talking about fishing. It's about how we live and work and how we use the Earth's resources in a way that gives us a decent life, while also making sure that we do not destroy the chance for future generations to enjoy similar benefits. Scotland has made great strides in trying to reduce its carbon emissions through renewable energy technology, even though personally I think the location of wind farms should have been much more carefully planned to protect Scotland's wild lands.

Richard Lochhead was in his post for some years and was in a good position to understand the challenges of using Scotland's land and sea wisely. But it's going to require real steel to make the long-term changes that are necessary to secure a sustainable future, where sustainability is to do with ecosystem health and not just our use of resources.

So what are the challenges facing any Minister for Rural Affairs? For a start, too much of Scotland's uplands are in a degraded state – as the next essay, 'The bonnie heather hills of Scotland', will show. Recently, there has been a lot of talk about rewilding and, because of the headline-grabbing nature of all media, this usually ends up with, 'When are the wolves arriving?' That's missing the point altogether. The big issue is that much more of Scotland – our farmlands, our forests, our uplands and our seas – must be in good ecological condition. That's what will help us in trying to meet the challenges of climate breakdown as well as ensuring that our land is capable of meeting the needs of our people in the long term.

# The bonnie heather hills of Scotland

When I first went to live in the Highlands of Scotland, in 1960, I was overwhelmed by the sense of space, the mountains and glens to roam and wide vistas stretching to the horizon to explore. I felt as though I had left the world behind, but I slowly realised that the purple blooming heather moors, lauded by tourists, were in fact an artificial landscape created by human activity. They were no different, in some ways, to the olive tree-dominated landscapes of southern Europe. That, though, has generally been a difficult concept for people to grasp, especially as those purple hills are an icon of Scottish tourism.

I was always an avid reader of older natural history books, such as James Ritchie's *The Influence of Man on Animal Life in Scotland*, and when I read Frank Fraser Darling's monumental *West Highland Survey* I reflected on his statement that 'the bald unpalatable fact is emphasised that the Highlands and Islands are largely a devastated terrain'. They are, in his words, a 'wet desert', a fact dramatically reinforced when I first went birding in the forests of New Hampshire. As I walked through beautiful, wild-looking woodlands listening to wood thrushes and phoebes, I came across old stone walls and the remains of buildings. My American companion explained to me that these lands were cleared of all trees by the first waves of European settlers to create farmland, but once the Europeans 'discovered' the inland great plains, much more suitable for agriculture, the hard farmlands of New England were abandoned. In no time, the trees returned and the pendulum that had once swung from woodland to 90 per cent cleared land had, within a century, swung back to continuous woodland.

I first met Fraser Darling when he was invited to open the new Nature Conservancy office in Inverness, and then had a few yarns with him in his study once he had moved, in old age, to live near Forres in Moray. I remember listening to his Reith lectures on the BBC in 1969 and hearing first-hand about the impacts of overgrazing around the world and in Scotland. In *Pelican in the Wilderness* he wrote of a 1950 field trip in New England:

> *On a visit to Harvard Forest, south of Athol, the country two hours south by train was not unlike Blair Atholl (in Scotland). Eighteenth-century settlement had given rise to a peak of farming activity in 1830–1840, and since 1850 there has been abandonment of farms, with the land going back to Forest. The pine, which has grown on this abandoned land, has been a beautiful even-aged stand of high quality. In Britain we have got the idea so firmly into our heads that land mistakenly taken from forest and no longer profitable in its mistaken use of farming or pastoralism must never go back to forest, that it would be sinful or a degradation to let it do so, and that we should organise subsidies to enable people to continue misuse of marginal land.*

And that's where, even now, we continue to be. Too much of upland Scotland is managed for single interests, and some of those are ecologically very damaging. Time and time again we have heard about the damaging impacts on Scotland of too many deer, too many sheep on poor land and large areas used solely for the shooting of red grouse. None of this is in the best interests of global ecosystems or our future.

Taking grouse moors as an example, ecological public focus is often on the issues of wildlife crime and, as someone who has had satellite-tracked raptors killed illegally, with no one brought to justice, you might think that that would be my principle gripe. I remember, though, the time in 2009 I went with the Angus police to search for and collect for analysis a poisoned golden eagle, which I had named Alma, on Milden Estate in Glenesk. I was just as alarmed, or even more so, by the intensive 'gardening' carried out by the keepers in the interests of grouse. I was shocked to see that ancient rowan trees growing along the burns had been cut down, so that crows could not nest nor raptors perch, with no recognition of the ecological importance of deciduous trees growing beside watercourses. It was botanical cleansing of the most severe form. I disliked the plethora of new roads for grouse management and shooting; and a regime based on burning surely has no long-term future in an age concerned with maintaining life on Earth. And – of course – I abhorred the illegal onslaught on raptors.

Heather moors may be beautiful in August, providing grouse to be shot by hunters and superb heather honey from bees, but they contribute very little to ecosystem functions. They don't aid water management and they don't help to build good soils, instead encouraging soil erosion. They don't produce much oxygen or store much carbon, as the same land would if regenerated with native trees, shrubs and plants. Even if we wish to keep red grouse hunting in the future, we must have a more equitable mix of moorland and woodland, and this will require a completely new look at how we manage the uplands and whether that management is for single interests or for society in general, especially in the long term.

In a modern-day Scotland the present regimes are unacceptable. It seems strange to me that anyone wanting to build a new house has to demonstrate their carbon-saving credentials in order to get planning permission, yet the owners of a huge grouse moor do not have to do an ecological audit of their activities. It's not that I dislike heather: to see the first flush of pink of the cross-leaved heath creeping across a bog or the bright purple of bell heather on a stony bank, then the hazy purple glow of ling heather stretching across the miles, is all part of the beauty of summer. It's more that there's just too much of it now.

The other great curse of the uplands is the dominance of open-range sheep farming. The original scrub and woodlands were, of course, mainly destroyed many centuries ago but that led to a pastoral agriculture based on small black cattle. Large numbers were herded to the hills and glens in summer from the low ground, and their non-selective grazing and dung created fertile environments, possibly mimicking the ancient effects of the long-exterminated wild native cattle called aurochs. Although our ancestors changed the land, they created many a fertile and productive landscape. As Fraser Darling said, 'The cattle husbandry and persistence of the forests were reasonably compatible and even complimentary, for the cattle received shelter from the forest and the trees benefited from the light cropping of the herbage floor, from the browsing and the manuring.'

In the industrial age sheep were more valuable than cattle, because of their wool, and the flock masters moved north with big sheep onto these excellent pastures, breaking the ancient ratio of one cow to one sheep. It's interesting to remember that in the 1780s the people of Easter Ross tried to turn back the first flocks of big sheep. In hindsight, theirs was an impossible dream. Turning again to Fraser Darling's words: 'The Coming of the Sheep caused much injury and destruction of forest by prevention of regeneration, but there were also directed attacks on the forests left by the smelters and timber companies. The brothers Stuart describe miles of pinewoods being burnt in Glenstrathfarrar in 1813 'to improve' the sheep pasture. There was at least one voice against – James Macdonald writing in 1811 – "The destroying of wood in every shape, or even inattention to the preservation of it, ought to be severely punished by persons of influence in this country."'

Tragically he was not heeded.

Again in *Pelican in the Wilderness*, Fraser Darling encapsulated the problem for the land: 'One thing much more obvious here (in North America) than at home (in Scotland) is that agricultural or pastoral prosperity means accelerated ill-treatment of the land. Such a remark made at home arouses hostility – I've tried it – because British farmers have the feeling that theirs is a calling suffused with righteousness "which would make it almost impossible for them to misuse land". This notion has been plugged so successfully that most folk overlook what the British farmer owes to an almost uniquely good climate. Lift that protective cloak and he has to exercise his mind a good deal more to remain a good farmer. Almost equally, of course, there is the other end of the stick – things going so badly that the ground has to be beaten to get a bare existence. Ideally it would seem that farming should be in such a state that only the best practice would yield profit. We haven't got there yet.' In my lifetime, much of upland farming has been the same, despite the fact there are well-run upland farms and crofts.

If unbroken heather moors are not in the best interests of Scotland's ecological potential, then miles and miles of hills overgrazed by sheep and often now turned to unproductive juncus rush are just as bad or worse. Both need immediate remedy, which will at the same time need to address the high numbers of red deer. Once more turning to Fraser Darling, after his pioneering studies of red deer around Dundonnell, his view was that red deer numbers in Scotland should not rise above 50,000. How that recommendation was ignored, as increasing densities of deer just made worse the overgrazing caused by sheep. I remember when, years ago, I was at a dinner in Inverness for the retirement of the Red Deer Commission's long-serving secretary. In his short speech he mentioned the fact that his Annual Report to government always encouraged the shooting estates to keep deer numbers under control. He then added that he always asked his wife to check over his report before publication, and that she had once observed: 'In every one of your reports you ask them to control numbers but each succeeding annual report shows an increase in red deer numbers – why is that?' By the end of the millennium there were well over 300,000 red deer in Scotland.

It is appalling that neither the government nor the people paid enough heed to James Ritchie or Frank Fraser Darling, and although there are now many changes and some great demonstrations of ecological recovery, such as Abernethy Forest and Glenfeshie, the bald truth is that our country is still a 'wet desert'. We have to change and have to recognise the urgency of changing, and it is essential that much more than half of our degraded moors and glens must be re-afforested as soon as possible. Only then will our descendants have a chance to live in a restored and healthy environment.

# The dangers of downpours

Friday 7th July 2017 was the most appalling day of rain; it started overnight and just kept bucketing down all day. By evening, the small river across from my house was a raging torrent, and as I looked out into the gloom before going to my warm bed, I just could not help but think of the female ospreys on their treetop nests trying to keep their young ones warm and alive. I was sure they would be absolutely soaked and would need to be really good mothers to keep the chicks sheltered. And the following day, the males would find it really difficult to find fish in the flooded murky waters. The next morning the rain was still pouring down and everywhere was flooded. At least I knew from the weather forecast that it was due to stop at midday, but the female ospreys didn't and just had to sit there, crouched over the young, open to the elements.

At midday it did stop. Within an hour there was a nice breeze, and soon the sun came out. In late afternoon I decided to go round and monitor the osprey eyries in the closest part of Moray to my house. At the first nest, B01, the male was perched in the sunshine on his favourite dead Scots pine branch and his mate was carefully feeding her young in the eyrie on top of a larch tree. Already their feathers were dry and he had obviously just brought in a fish. The young at this nest were under a week old so I could see her putting tiny bits of fish down into the nest, but I did not see the chicks themselves. At the next site, the female stretched her wings above the nest, before flying off to bring back a small stick, which she added to her big eyrie and then shuffled back to keep her brood warm.

Next stop, and it was domestic bliss in the tall tree by a barley field; the female feeding young and her mate perched on the side of the nest. He, again, must have just brought home a fish. It was beautiful watching them through my telescope against the evening sun.

I next checked on Morven, an old well-known female that was the last one to lay eggs in this area. When I telescoped her nest from my car I could not see anything, but then the white top of her head poked above the nest edge. She was sitting tight, incubating eggs and keeping very low down.

At the next eyrie, the earliest breeder in this area, the chicks must have been recently fed, for they were lying quiet in the nest while their mother stood on the edge, preening her feathers. My final visit was to the eyrie used for many years by Beatrice; the new female there was sitting high in the nest and she was brooding very small young.

Six pairs of ospreys, and all had come safely through the appalling weather – I'm told we had two inches of rain in twenty-four hours. These female ospreys really have to put up with some bad conditions in Scotland and I'm always impressed by how well they protect their young from very heavy rain. What I do know, though, is that if heavy rain continues for more than two days and nights, young ospreys do die in their nests. A few years ago, I remember six complete broods died due to three days and nights of rain. Thankfully, this time, there was a happier ending.

# Traditional cattle and biodiversity

One of my most satisfying times, as a crofter in the 1990s, was driving, or rather walking behind, a herd of our cattle heading for the summer pastures. I always felt peace and contentment moving them – although sometimes touched with anxiety when passing a neighbour's dodgy fence – as though I'd been doing this for a thousand years. It was pure bliss in a mad world. At times the cows were silent, except for the hurried snatching of mouthfuls of grass from the roadside, but would then start bawling when they saw a neighbour's cows. But the older cows, all known by name, knew that at the end of the day's walk of three miles – in the old days it was called transhumance – were fields of grass and a thousand acres of hill-grazing with woods. The calves scampered to keep up. At that time we had a herd of twenty-five Aberdeen Angus cross beef cows for producing high quality beef stirks, sold for fattening on the lowland farms. These cows were low intensive, natural fed and not treated with avermectins for internal parasites.

Several thousand years ago, the wild cattle, or aurochs, of Europe would have grazed these same lands. The occasional skull or bones are still found in the peat. Early man then arrived with small black cattle, domesticated from aurochs in the eastern Mediterranean region. Later called kyloes, these small black Highland cattle were the mainstay of the peoples living in the Scottish Highlands. Thousands were taken to upland summer grazings from the low ground farms and crofts; it was said the grass might be knee-high in the Cairngorms when they arrived in late spring. The women and children, living in remote sheilings, made butter and cheese from the rich milk through the summer and early autumn. We can still see the outlines of their circular sheilings in our hills and imagine the sounds of dozens of playing children in the evening light and the bluey drift of smoke from their cooking fires.

Those traditional cattle enhanced the land in a most astonishing way because of their non-specialised grazing; their dung and urine also fertilised the land, and they left behind a network of tracks. The cattle recycled plant material, thus increasing plant biomass and diversifying plant communities. This kind of grazing on extensive pastures, near enough replicating that of aurochs, was very sympathetic with nature and enhanced biodiversity wonderfully. Their tragic loss to make way for myriad sheep more than two hundred years ago, and the more recent impacts of too many red deer – both animals are selective grazers – has resulted in the removal of that fertility, as well as a tragic loss of plant diversity and thus massive ecological degradation. We're back again to that 'wet desert' of Fraser Darling.

From watching hill cattle in Abernethy Forest, I have seen that their grazing keeps glades and flushes open, maintains flower meadows and trims the willow scrub. Their dung constitutes an effective method of spreading plant seeds, and it is a valuable habitat for invertebrates, which are important food for many birds and mammals. Annually, a cow not only produces about four tons of dung but the pats harbour an annual insect population weighing about a quarter of her own body weight. That, though, is true only when the cows have not been treated with chemicals like avermectins. I find it tragic to look at the cowpats in most fields of commercial cattle, for they are nowadays too toxic for insects to colonise.

Some say we must reduce cattle numbers because of the impact of methane emissions on global warming, but traditional cattle living on open range, with a multi-species diet, create far less methane than commercial cattle fed on intensive grasslands and silage.

Traditional cattle are an integral part of the natural environment and its native fauna. To lose them is to lose a major player in the ecology of the Scottish hills and forests. To me, nature conservation is more than just the protection of species or habitats: it is to do with life on Earth. It is the optimum use of the sun's energy to create plant biomass, which in turn is eaten and digested by herbivores, and thus by carnivores and secondary carnivores. Simply, it is the food chain, although in reality it is an incredibly complex array of life and death support systems with which we are inextricably linked. At this point in time, we badly need to have more of Scotland in prime ecological condition. My premise is that it is impossible to restore our natural forest and moorland ecosystems to full vigour without cattle, one of the most beneficially influential herbivores. Alongside beavers, moose, lynx, wolf, bear and wild boar, they were a key species in the primeval Scottish forests.

Successful nature conservation is a skilful blend of experience, observation, knowledge and perception, rather than solely a science. It requires a strong working partnership between experienced country folk, administrators, conservationists and scientists to make the principles of large ecosystem management work well on the ground.

# Lynx kittens in my pockets

In 2000, at a joint WWF meeting of the large herbivore and large carnivore initiatives in Spain's Cantabrian Mountains, I spoke with a Norwegian friend, Reidar Andersen, about his studies on roe deer, lynx and red fox. His project involved radio tagging young lynx in the field, and I was so envious that I asked to join him the following summer. 'I'll be in touch!' said Reidar.

I got an email in June 2001. 'It's on, get yourself to Oslo for 7th July.' I replied that I was happy to drive further north as I knew that he lived in Trondheim and I was sure the lynx were living in wild country well north of the capital. But I was collected at the airport terminal and, to my amazement, driven maybe half an hour outside Oslo. We followed a track north into a forest and, before long, found Reidar's colleagues; they had located a radio-tagged female and were certain the den was in a rock scree close by in the forest. We drove half a kilometre further and met two fieldworkers. The female lynx was growling above us on the wooded hillside and a search was made in the big jumble of rocks; finally, two kittens were found hidden under a big rock in a comfortable den. They were so beautiful and I was totally knocked out. I was allowed to hold them and after biometrics had been taken, along with blood samples, they were put back into their secure den. I just wished I could have hidden them in my pockets and taken them home to Scotland.

After supper at the field station, we set off to radio track a tagged male lynx. The forest was interspersed with small farms growing cereals and grass and keeping some livestock. We could see the glow of the city lights not far away. In the dusk we had seen several roe deer grazing in the fields and then Reidar picked up the signals of the lynx. We were able to track its route along the edge of a small farm, very similar to the croft where I lived in Strathspey. We were parked on a local road, armed with a strong torch, and saw something behind us; we swivelled round to see a fox cross the road. Sadly, while we were looking that way, the lynx crossed the road in front of us. I didn't see him but I learned a lot, principally that lynx could easily live in Scotland and that it was a disgrace that we were unable to restore this beautiful and iconic predator to our country.

Earlier, in 1988, when I was still working for the RSPB, I was heavily involved in the purchase of Abernethy Forest. It was a major challenge for the Society to take on such a huge area of wonderful nature conservation land. There were big challenges ahead and the major one was to hugely reduce the damage caused by too many red and roe deer. It was my task to open the batting on this delicate subject by giving a lecture on the new Abernethy Forest reserve to the RSPB Members' Annual Conference in York. It was a difficult message I had to pass on: 'We've got to kill a lot of deer.' It was at this time that I really started to push the message that in order for our big nature reserves to work properly we had to restore the big lost mammals – beaver, wild boar and lynx – and even contemplate wolf and brown bear.

In May 1994, I appeared in court in Germany as part of a prosecution of two German falconers who had stolen peregrine eggs in the Scottish Highlands. After the case I took the opportunity to find and meet experts on lynx, wolf and brown bear at the Munich Wildlife Society field station in the mountains. I had a wonderful couple of days and became hooked, as I now had real knowledge and knew skilled ecologists who could supply expert advice and answers. Later, in December, I was at Aberdeen airport collecting two of these experts, Professor Wolfgang Schroeder and Dr Christoph Promberger. I drove them over the high roads by way of the Lecht and they were shocked at the state of a land devoid of its original tree cover. We had an excellent three days in the field visiting Abernethy Forest and other locations north to Glen Affric. Their parting message, back at the airport, was that Scotland had excellent areas, large enough for all three species. There were no ecological barriers to successful reintroductions; it was solely a matter of social and political will. It's remained that way ever since. Twenty-five years on, we are no nearer bringing back the predators. It's not something I'm proud of when I talk about conservation issues in foreign countries. Come on, let's get it done!

# Insect Armageddon

One evening in 2017, I had a phone call at home from LBC radio in London. The producer asked if I would talk with Clive Bull about the 'Insect Armageddon' story that had been trending in the news. Why me? I guessed at this hour that I was the only one to be found. Fortunately, I had looked at the report by scientists on the 75 per cent reduction in flying insects on ninety-three German nature reserves between 1989 and 2016, so I did know the story (see the paper in the journal *Plos One*).

I also felt strongly connected to this news, as I am old enough to remember car trips to the New Forest in the 1950s when, after twenty miles or so, you'd have to scrape the windscreen clear of dead insects and, from time to time, clear the radiator grille. That was also true in the Scottish Highlands in the 1960s. Just guess what the reduction of flying insects really has been in the UK if you used 1950 or 1960 as the baseline, rather than 1989. It's truly disastrous.

Ornithologists are used to the severity of the declines: think of 97 per cent of turtle doves gone since 1970. When I recently heard some singing in Andalucía, it reminded me of my childhood in rural Hampshire. What a loss to our enjoyment of the countryside it has been to lose that gentle purring in the hawthorn hedges. Look, too, at the appalling loss of grey partridges, corn buntings, yellowhammers, poppies, corn cockles and marigolds due to the great changes in agricultural practice since the 1960s. Ian Newton's brilliant *Farming and Birds* (part of the New Naturalist series) explores the whole history of farming and birds, and the relationships – both good and bad – between the two. It details fully the dramatic changes due to the intensification of farming and the onslaught of a bewildering array of chemicals – insecticides, herbicides, fungicides and artificial fertilisers – which has led to the loss of wild plants, insects and soil ecosystems. Although individual chemicals are tested for impacts, the real problem is the cocktail of chemicals from agriculture added to emissions from industry and the way we live, including acid rain.

It shocks me that scientific reports document the impacts on wildlife and the threat to the future global ecosystems, yet society seems unable to rein back the worst aspects of intensive agriculture. When I started working with wildlife in the early 1960s, the immediate worry was the rapid declines of raptors such as peregrines and golden eagles. Scientists proved this was due to new chemicals being used in sheep dips and agriculture. The conservation bodies, government and NGOs demanded change and within a reasonable time they were taken out of use and the problems subsided. Why are demands for change not met nowadays? Are the conservation bodies less able or organised, are the politicians more negligent or are the chemical companies and the farming industry much stronger?

My very strong view is that we need immediate change rather than more research. Governments and big business love research: it means they don't have to do anything now. And nature, if given a chance, can bounce back.

# A good day with red squirrels

On the last day of August 2015, my fieldwork was with red squirrels rather than ospreys. It was a magical day. At noon, I called in on old friends at Amat Estate in Sutherland to see how the squirrels in their woodlands had done. We sat at the kitchen table looking out at their bird table above the river. Soon there was one squirrel, then another, and in the end a total of seven beautiful red squirrels, all of them, bar one, born in 2015.

This area was where we, the Highland Foundation for Wildlife, working with The European Nature Trust and the landowners and staff of Alladale, Amat and Croick estates, translocated thirty-six red squirrels that I had caught in Moray and Strathspey during February and March 2013.

When I left the house I saw three more in the gardens and another ran across the public road as I drove off. Eleven squirrels – no wonder my friends said to me how much they loved the project and what pleasure so many visitors had gained from our successful work to restore red squirrels to this part of the Highlands, where they had died out nearly fifty years before. Two really young squirrels had also recently been seen in the nearby Alladale pinewoods and, judging by the number of eaten pine cones on the forest floor that I witnessed, red squirrels were indeed alive and well there also.

Later in the day, after checking out a satellite-tagged golden eagle location, I drove along Loch Broom from Ullapool. It was great to know that those pinewoods also had red squirrels again. In the winter of 2008 and 2009, I organised and carried out our first translocation of red squirrels under a licence from Scottish Natural Heritage. This pioneering project was carried out with the enthusiasm and support of Dundonnell Estate. We moved forty-three red squirrels from Moray and Strathspey, with the support of private landowners and people who feed squirrels in their gardens.

Two squirrels were live trapped in any one place, checked by Jane Harley, a Strathspey vet, and then driven the same day to the release site. Each squirrel was transported in a nest box containing hay, nuts and sweet apple, and the boxes were fixed in trees in groups of four at the release site in Dundonnell woodlands. At each site six nut feeders were also erected and these were kept restocked during the first winter by Alasdair MacDonald, the estate keeper. Young squirrels were observed in the first summer and the population grew rapidly, with one enterprising squirrel even walking over the mountains to Leckmelm, near Ullapool. The owners of the garden reported to me that it was male, so in March 2009 I released a female in the same garden, and that spring they bred and reared young. The local people thought it was magic – a bit like a 'lonely hearts' club' for squirrels! I called there again in January 2020 and my friends, John and Ann, told me that their garden was still a haven for squirrels.

The translocation of red squirrels to Dundonnell was so successful that in March 2012 we moved twenty more from Dundonnell to three private estates on Loch Broomside. Again, the squirrels responded, and it's wonderful to know that red squirrels have spread throughout all the available woodlands and now occur in some of the gardens in Ullapool. The squirrels were last seen in these parts of Wester Ross in the 1960s and 1970s, and it's very satisfying to think there are probably now between 500 and 1,000 squirrels between Dundonnell and Ullapool. At the Sutherland site, red squirrels have spread ten miles or more down the glen, and I received a wonderful eyewitness account of a squirrel boldly swimming across the River Carron to get to conifers on the other side of the water. By 2018, they had reached Rosehall and Strathoykell. It's been very exciting to see how well these wonderful wee creatures have responded, given the chance.

That's why I then had discussions with SNH and was granted a five-year licence to carry out further translocations in the Scottish Highlands, north and west of the present range. It's a great way to create new populations isolated from the threat of grey squirrels and their disease risk. Under the licence, Trees for Life are also carrying out a series of translocations to suitable locations. My foundation has also more recently successfully restored red squirrels to Inverewe Gardens in Wester Ross and to Loch Ossian in Lochaber. I think our pioneering fieldwork has been so successful that it should be copied in many areas of mainland UK, instead of just accepting the presence of grey squirrels.

# Sea eagles on Sunday

My friend Mike Crutch of A9 Birding invited me to join him and two Inverness birders, Sam and Debbie, on a day trip to Skye to photograph sea eagles. Although I have been involved in the reintroduction and conservation of white-tailed eagles since 1968 at Fair Isle, I'd never actually been on a boat trip to feed them.

In August 2017, the weather had been poor, until a brief calm period was forecast for a Sunday at the end of the month. As we drove through the Ross-shire mountains, the skies were clear and our arrival at Carbost pier revealed a calm sea. Soon the *MV Wild Skye* left the pier and was heading through Loch Harport, with a distant view of a sea eagle, before passing the lighthouse and aiming for a section of the great western cliffs of the Isle of Skye. It was a perfect morning. We could see the hills of the Uists away over The Minch and two porpoises broke the glassy surface.

We motored to the main cliffs where we very quickly found a pair of sea eagles and their exceptional brood of three flying young. This pair of eagles, like many others around the coasts, learnt early on that fishing boats are good for scraps to eat. The first eagles might have learnt by watching gulls scavenging dead fish as lobster fishermen checked and reset their creels. In the 1990s, Portree boatmen realised that the eagles would come down for fish thrown from their boats, and so sea eagle tourism was born, giving people incredible views of these great birds and excellent opportunities for photography.

The boat engine was stopped and we could hear the young eagles calling. The adults were looking down from the cliffs as they knew full well what would happen next. When the skipper threw a fish away from the boat, the male plunged from the cliffs and, in a sweep of huge wings, grabbed the food from the water to the noise of camera shutters. What a fantastic sight! It was something I never foresaw when I released those first four young Norwegian sea eagles on Fair Isle in 1968. Close-up sea eagle viewing has become one of the most exciting wildlife experiences in modern-day Scotland.

There were no sea eagles when I first visited Skye in the early 1960s but I knew of their sad history. The nineteenth-century naturalist and author John Alexander Harvie-Brown recorded the history of persecution and extinction, as well as the visit in 1868 to this very cliff by a Victorian collector who took two eggs and shot an adult eagle. How times have changed. There are now more than 140 pairs of white-tailed sea eagles in Scotland; they are admired and enjoyed by thousands of people, locals and visitors. And with sea eagle tourism reportedly bringing in £5 million a year to the island of Mull, they contribute remarkably to jobs and income in fragile rural communities.

# The invader from the Orient

On 28th August 1960, I was heading for Aberdeen to catch the ferry to Shetland and decided to call by Covesea Farm, near Lossiemouth. A bird-watching friend had told me that collared doves, a very rare bird from the East, had nested there and I was sure to see them if I called in and spoke to the farmer, Mr Adam. Sure enough, in the front garden of his house, which was a small wood of cypresses, I saw my first collared dove in Scotland. In fact, my diary reminds me that I saw ten at close range and in flight; they were displaying and calling 'screoo-screoo', not unlike a guinea fowl, and I made a note of their plumage and of the fact that they were bigger than turtle doves. There was a pied flycatcher in the trees as well.

It's difficult to think that this now-common bird was once so rare. Between 1930 and 1960, the collared dove staged an incredible 1,000-mile north-west colonisation of Europe from Yugoslavia. In 1955, they started to breed in Norfolk, and I remember a few years later, in January 1960, visiting Cromer to get the species on my life list. That year they reached Fair Isle as a migrant for the first time, and that north-westerly urge continued with the first records in the Faroe Islands and in Iceland in 1964. Why this species suddenly exploded on a north-west invasion is not known; was there a genetic change that spurred it on? I guess we will never know, but that's the magic of wildlife.

Returning to Moray, where I now live, the first nesting pair was recorded in a garden in June 1958. One young was reared, the first for Scotland. In 1959, they reared four young and by 1960 the population was seventeen. In autumn 1961, I counted thirty-five, perched on wires and the TV aerial. Collared doves then started to spread very slowly, at first preferring to stay where they first settled.

One summer day in 1962, I was on watch at the osprey observation hide at Loch Garten, where I worked for the RSPB. We had two keen birdwatchers from Glasgow volunteering for a week, and they had never seen a collared dove. I told them a pair had moved in 1960 to Forres in Moray, less than an hour up the road, so off we set in the early evening and found our way to a big house with ornamental gardens on the east side of the town. The owner, Douglas Cowie, was really welcoming and said we should sit in the drawing room whilst his wife threw some maize on to the lawn. The birds, he said, knew her much better. Our host showed us to the best seats by the big windows and made life even better with welcome drams of malt whisky. In no time, several collared doves fluttered down onto the lawn and my friends added the bird to their life lists. 'That's the real way to see a new bird!' they said, as we drove away. That autumn Mr Cowie counted twenty-seven at his home.

In 1964, I called again at Mr Adam's farm and saw about 200 doves perched along the wires above his cattle sheds, and on 8th February 1972 they peaked at 328. I'm afraid his opinion of the rare doves was changing, as they fed eagerly on the cereals meant for his cattle. Not long after that, the species spread out across the countryside and it was not long before predators had worked out this new addition to our fauna, bringing the bird to a more natural population level. Now you can see them in most towns and villages, but in quite small numbers. They are still in Forres and Covesea, but there are rarely more than a handful together. In fact, in the new century, the species has started to decline and I guess now most people do not know the amazing history of this common bird of our towns and gardens.

# Quiet pride over red kites

We were in the south for a wedding near Rutland Water and to see family in Hampshire and Buckinghamshire. Driving on motorways or back roads, we saw red kites as the most common raptor above our heads. The first of them showed up in the grey autumn skies as we headed for my son Roddy's home in Amersham, with more on the way south to Hampshire and north to Stamford. One morning we walked into Old Amersham through lovely beech woods, kites overhead – even one patrolling the road where my son lived. I reflected on this dramatic change in my lifetime, when once they were restricted to mid-Wales.

That's what I like about kites: they are so easy to see and identify with their distinctive forked tails. They also respond so well to human contact. I find it marvellous that people can now feed red kites in their back gardens. The remains of a chicken leg here or an old sausage there make a welcome meal for this ultimate scavenger. I'm generally not keen on feeding birds and have always felt uneasy about the huge amounts of non-native food, such as peanuts, that are fed to birds in Britain. I'm not sure it's in their long-term interest and I also think it obscures the appalling declines of common birds due to intensive agriculture, chemicals and the pressures of modern life. But feeding red kites is different: they have fed beside humans right back to our earliest ancestors. For early man, as well as Neanderthals, it would have been an everyday event to see kites swooping down for morsels at ancient campsites or after hunts for large mammals. It's lovely to think that they would once have fed on scraps of woolly mammoth or woolly rhino being cut up by humans in ancient Britain. Nowadays there is such a rush to clean up dead animals in the countryside that the supply of carrion is really limited for birds like kites. We are, alas, too tidy and the ecosystem functions break down.

Whenever a kite floated over, I took quiet pride in the fact that twenty-five years ago, no kites bred in England or Scotland, and that I was fortunate to be one of the RSPB and Nature Conservancy team that restored the species. In June 1989, after a good few years of opposition and delay to my proposal to reintroduce red kites to the Scottish Highlands, I flew to southern Sweden on the very first kite-collecting trip. Ornithological friends in Lund were hugely helpful to me. They set up my base at the University field station and the next morning we visited our first nests, on nearby military ranges, to find broods of three or even four young kites. Each evening over the four days, after busy and hectic hours of tree climbing, ringing and collecting, I spent my time cutting up meat and fish to feed the increasing groups of young kites.

Once we had collected twelve young, we were ready to start what has become an incredibly successful project. The young birds and I were driven from Sweden to Denmark, via the ferry, and then onwards to a Danish military base. Once there, an RAF Nimrod patrol aircraft from Kinloss swooped in to take me back to northern Scotland with my precious cargo. Eight of the young kites were reared and released at a friend's farm close to my home on the Black Isle near Inverness and the other four travelled south overnight to the Chilterns release area.

Over the next four summers I returned to Skåne County every June to collect more kites from the beautiful woods, where I could hear icterine warblers and thrush nightingales. A total of ninety-three red kites were translocated to Scotland. When I left the RSPB, others continued the project elsewhere in England and Scotland with kites from Spain and Germany. Our initiative became one of the most successful reintroduction projects ever, with red kites now breeding from northern Scotland down through many parts of the UK to the south of England, meaning that this distinctively shaped raptor once again circles town and countryside.

How I wish that we could get on and see golden eagles and sea eagles, too, over such a big range. It's perfectly easy to do, ecologically, but in the UK, bold ideals are far too often hampered by social and political concerns. But remember: it's never 'if', it's always 'when'.

# Thoughts on wild red grouse

The red grouse is one of the most distinctive birds of the British Isles and has in the past been regarded as a separate species (*Lagopus scotica*) to the willow grouse (*Lagopus lagopus*) of mainland Europe. In earlier times it was the UK's only endemic bird species. Now, even though it is only regarded as a subspecies of the willow grouse, it is distinctively different in plumage characteristics as well as in habitat and food preferences.

Evidence from mitochondrial DNA implies that willow grouse and red grouse have actually been distinct for much longer than 10,000 years and Lucchini, writing in 2001, tentatively suggested that the Swedish and Scottish grouse differ by 3.13 per cent in their cytochrome b gene. Derek Yalden goes on to say that the average reported rate of tetraonine gene change might suggest red and willow grouse have been separated for 433,000 years rather than 10,000 years, and that their distinctiveness may have survived at least four glacial/interglacial sequences, with respective refuges being in Iberia and the Balkans. There is every chance that red grouse will some day be regarded once more as a separate species, which it surely is, and thus be endemic to the British Isles.

Red grouse have been managed for sport shooting for nearly 200 years, but the rate of intervention has increased considerably in recent decades in order to increase and maintain high 'bags' for hunters and income for landowners. Controlled heather burning has been practised for most of this time, while intensive predator control has been the norm, often including, since the middle of the last century, the illegal killing of raptors, thus removing some of the natural mortality influences. Recent advances in technology means that keepers can also use thermal imaging equipment for controlling foxes; and, in the wrong hands, that same technology may be used for illegally killing raptors at night. Present-day red grouse management can also involve habitat management and simplification, such as the removal of all trees and bushes, including juniper. It may also involve the near eradication of blue hares because of competition, disease risk and to reduce prey for wandering golden eagles.

On some grouse moors, red and roe deer are greatly reduced or eliminated to prevent perceived problems with ticks and louping ill disease in red grouse. In recent times, sheep have been used as 'tick mops' to kill ticks using regular applications (as many as six per summer) of acaricidal insecticides. It doesn't sound much fun for the sheep. For the last twenty years or so, most grouse moors have been equipped with medicated grit sites so that grouse can be treated with anthelmintic chemicals to control strongyle worm infestations. Many estates carry out intensive programmes of live capturing of red grouse in the winter months, using spot lights and hand nets at night, so that they can be dosed with anthelmintics. On some estates, this may mean the capture of up to 90 per cent of the grouse per winter. Some grouse have been fitted with acraricidal leg bands.

Red grouse numbers have been kept at high levels in many regions through these intensive methods, with little or no cycling of population numbers, as in past times. The natural cycling of grouse may have long-term benefits to the species, while any impacts of these treatments on other wildlife, such as raptors, is unknown. Recent outbreaks of mycoplasma and cryptosporidium have been thought to be due to high densities of grouse concentrating at medicated grit sites and passing on diseases. This might be increasing the risk of disease spread to other wildlife. There have also been reports that high numbers of red grouse, still present after the shooting season, have been caught up and transferred to other estates, including reports of red grouse being moved from northern England to Sutherland.

The red grouse is such a special UK bird species that it must be important to consider whether some of these practices are putting at risk the long-term evolutionary processes of such an important wild bird. The EU Council Directive 2009/147/EC on the conservation of wild birds requires the UK to take the requisite measures for the protection of the red grouse. The species is on the Joint Nature Conservation Committee (JNCC) species priority list, version 2, but intrusive management is not highlighted in the actions list.

It would appear judicious, if these intrusive practices continue, that sufficiently large populations are allowed to live in 'near natural' conditions throughout the regional distribution in the UK. This must not just be in low-density unmanaged areas but also in high-density populations on the best soils. These measures are needed in order to ensure the long-term evolution and survival of red grouse. As an immediate step there should be a suite of Special Protection Areas, or zones of 'no chemical treatments', specifically for our most distinctive endemic bird to live in near natural conditions and habitats. And while we are at it, let's make it a full species again.

# Big fish

In 1959, when I lived on the remote Fair Isle, between Orkney and Shetland, I remember the islanders fishing from their distinctive open boats, catching superb haddock, cod and ling for home consumption. There's nothing better to eat than a fish straight out of the ocean. In those days, there were no deep freezes and the fish not immediately eaten were gutted, salted and dried outdoors for the winter. Back then, the islanders still collected seabird eggs, and sponge cakes were even more delicious if someone had been to the guillemot nesting colonies. During the Second World War, seabirds and their eggs were important parts of the islanders' diet, and they also shot shags around the cliffs, sending them off to England for sale as 'black ducks'. Unsurprisingly, the shag became an extremely shy and wary bird.

At that time there was a three-nautical-mile limit, protecting inshore waters from trawlers, and – from 1964 – a twelve-mile limit, which kept out foreign fishing boats. Peter Davis, the warden of the Fair Isle bird observatory, had worked as the warden on Lundy Island in the 1950s, when the eccentric owner of the island had given the bird observatory a .303 rifle to fire at French fishing boats to stop them coming and taking lobsters close to the island. By the time I was there, in 1958, that tradition had ceased and we established good relations with the Breton crabbers, swapping fresh vegetables and eggs for a bottle of Dubonnet and some Gauloises cigarettes.

At Fair Isle, the inshore waters were reserved for traditional, small-boat fishing, which could sometimes be spectacularly good. I went out once with three young islanders who had set a long line of baited hooks in the tidal streams south of the island. As they hauled it in, we saw that they had caught several big skate. Suddenly, all hell let loose as they pulled on board a massive halibut weighing much more than any of us, at 80 kilograms. After what I thought was a fearsome scrum, with me seeking shelter in the bow, it was successfully tied below the thwarts. Their luck was in, for they then pulled in another, only slightly smaller, to complete a fantastic day's fishing. The two big halibut were sent off on a passing trawler for auction in Aberdeen fish market.

The protected zones were scrapped by Margaret Thatcher's government in 1984, which led to the progressive over-fishing of our inshore waters. This was clearly a bad decision for indigenous coastal people like the Fair Islanders, who lost exclusive access to a ready supply of good fish for themselves, either fresh or dried for the winter, while their traditional fishing places were gradually degraded.

I returned to live on Fair Isle for seven years from 1963, during a period that saw a massive onslaught on herring and mackerel in the North Sea by a whole range of fishing nations. We used to look out from the island at night and see the lights of what looked like a city to the east. During the day, the source of the lights would become clear: a fleet of trawlers scooping up the great shoals of fish with massive purse nets. The catchers were accompanied by huge factory ships to process the fish. Stories abound of boats so laden with herring and mackerel that they were close to sinking on their way back to Norway, where the whole crew were able to buy the latest model Volvo or BMW. Fortunes were made and it was no wonder that these two species collapsed. That collapse was, in fact, so spectacular that some African nations, annoyed at others highlighting the killing of elephants, suggested that the herring should become a specially protected species under international law.

During the 1960s, Fair Isle's breeding seabirds continued to boom, probably due to a massive increase of small fish following the collapse of the larger ones, which were their normal predators. The seabirds' breeding grounds on Fair Isle became specially protected by our own laws and by the designation of an EU Special Protection Area for birds. But the birds' feeding areas at sea did not have any level of protection. There have always been two problems: we tend to view the sea as an endless resource and fishermen do not like restrictions. There seems to be a gut feeling that 'if I don't take the fish, someone else will, so it might as well be me'. It's called the problem of 'commons' and serves as a bit of an excuse to duck the issues.

Nowadays, scientists have shown that the North Sea has warmed up since the 1960s and the important sand eel species has moved north, making it less available to birds like puffins and kittiwakes. The big recovery in mackerel and herring has probably impacted the small fish as well. The seabird declines have been dramatic. Some years ago I went back to Fair Isle in spring to make a BBC2 documentary film about seabirds, and I was shocked to see the old kittiwake nesting cliffs and to hear nothing. The scurrying flocks of birds collecting nest material from the tops of the cliffs, calling incessantly, which I had known so well, had gone.

In the early 1990s, as a board member of the newly formed Scottish Natural Heritage, the Scottish successor to the UK-wide Nature Conservancy Council, I asked for clarification on our role. Did our remit on the conservation of species extend to the international 200-mile limit, and was the conservation of cod and halibut equal to the conservation of golden eagle and wildcat? Our chairman, Magnus Magnusson, assured me that it was. Not long after, I was a member of the newly established Marine Task Force, which I found extremely illuminating. On a visit to Aberdeen, I remember the professor in charge of the Torry Research Station explaining the then present-day age ratios of fish in the North Sea. His comparison? To imagine walking down the city's Union Street and seeing no human over the age of seven years old. It was worse than I expected: there was a real problem in our seas but we were not even going to help solve it, because the work of our task force was curtailed by government and the fledgling report buried. We were, in essence, told to go back and worry about golden eagles and wildcats.

That was a big mistake, though, because we have heard so often the fishermen say they are the best guardians of the seas. I remember, when I presented a BBC2 film on Britain's seabirds, that to ensure balance within the programme I interviewed a member of the Shetland Fishermen's Association. His first comments were, 'I don't understand Roy's concerns about Fair Isle because we don't fish there.' At the end of the interview I asked what would happen if big stocks of fish were to appear in Fair Isle waters. He replied, 'We'd fish them.' Well, the French fishermen and others did that to the orange roughy, which was discovered in the early 1990s living on sub-oceanic mountaintops off north-west Scotland. Some of these 60-centimetre-long fish were 150 years old and needed to live to about thirty years before they bred. In 1991, the fishermen caught 5,000 tonnes in the first year, at a rate only a fisherman would say was sustainable. I remember our discussing this problem within Scottish Natural Heritage and the UK view seemed to be that our fishermen must join the race, at least to allow them to get a quota when controls came in. A decade later, the orange roughies were so scarce that they were no longer there to fish. At about that time I read Charles Clover's seminal book *The End of the Line*, which outlined the true impact of the fishing industry throughout the world's oceans. I could only read a chapter at a time because it was so distressing.

Similarly, but on another scale, I joined my daughter Rona in 1994 on her fieldwork on tropical forest conservation in the amazing headwaters of the Kapuas River in West Kalimantan,

Indonesia, where she was an expert on forest fire systems. One day, following the river, we turned a corner to find the waterway blocked with boats. Our local guide stopped and talked with a friend. A gorgeous yellow and black-banded fish, new to that wetland, had been discovered in this tiny area; the locals were getting something like $1 for each, while the traders sold them at the coastal town of Pontianak for about $10. Goodness knows what each fish cost then to aquarium enthusiasts in the United States. I passed that way three years later and not a single boat was present. The fish were gone.

I understand about climate breakdown and warming seas but I, like many other ecologists, still remain certain that the present control of fisheries in the world is woefully inadequate. In Scotland, no matter what the Scottish and UK government or the EU suggests, it's nearly always wrong from the fishing industry's point of view. Discussions about wise use for the future are difficult because of the history of fishing, a dangerous occupation in which lives have frequently been lost. There are also the arguments about whose fish they are. Do they belong to the fishermen and, if they do, do they belong to local fishermen, Scottish fishermen, UK fishermen, EU fishermen or any old fishermen? Or do they belong to the people of Scotland, if in fact they do belong to anyone? I think that the management of the marine environment and its resources in Scottish waters should be managed by the government of Scotland for the benefit of the Earth's marine environment and the Scottish people.

Clearly the fishermen are key players in this debate and it is essential that we have a successful fishing industry in Scotland. It must, though, be the aim of our government to ensure that it is managed in a way that also optimises the long-term benefits for the marine ecosystem and for future generations of fishermen. There are already many conflicts, with local fishermen complaining about larger boats, about scallop dredging, and with arguments raging between langoustine creeling and dredging for 'scampi'. Additionally, there are complaints about the fishing industry's impacts on the marine ecosystem, on fish conservation, on the seabeds and the food of Scotland's seabirds.

My view is that we have reached a critical point, and that half – and I truly mean 50 per cent, by area – of the world's seas and oceans, including those of Scotland, should never be fished. Fishing exclusion zones should be established to allow fish to prosper and spread along our coasts and out into deep water. In between these zones would be fishing zones to provide food for humans. It's a method that's known to work as there are already some successful stories around the world – for example, New Zealand – so Scotland urgently needs to follow suit, and in a significant way. Designation for designation's sake is not enough: it must really work for sea fish communities and ecosystems within our waters.

# Autumn

# Rabbits – here today, gone tomorrow

When I was a boy at Scout camp on a hill farm inland from Machynlleth, in mid-Wales, I gained my backwoodsman's badge. For this I had to set wire snares to trap a wild rabbit on the farm, then gut it, skin it and cook it over an open fire. We ate it for supper. When I got home my mum sewed my badge on the sleeve of my Scout shirt. Then came myxomatosis in the mid-1950s, people went off eating rabbits, and rabbit numbers crashed to near extinction levels. Farmers enjoyed the respite from crop damage, and buzzards and other rabbit predators suffered and declined in numbers. The southern downlands, home of stone curlews, rare butterflies and orchids, lost much of their open grassland to scrub. Rabbits slowly gained immunity and from then on fluctuated with the disease.

Rabbits on many of the offshore islands did not suffer from myxomatosis and often they were incredibly plentiful. On Lundy Island, when I lived there in 1958, rabbits were everywhere and ravens would follow us when we went out with a .22 rifle to shoot some rabbits for the pot; they would swoop down to eat the gut remains after we left. If we went birding in the same spot with just our binoculars, the ravens did not follow.

Interestingly, the ancestors of those rabbits on Lundy Island go back a thousand years to the time when French nobles were the first people to bring rabbits to Britain. They reared them for food and fur in warrens on offshore islands free of large predators. Some people suggest that the Romans brought rabbits to Britain, but those ones were domesticated and apparently did not escape into the countryside. The later rabbits did very well and were recognised as a great food, soon being reared in protected warrens on many mainland estates.

## Rabbits – here today, gone tomorrow

The rabbit trade in Britain before myxomatosis was massive. Older keepers have told me of trapping a couple of thousand rabbits per winter on estates in the Highlands and sending them off by train to London every evening. Rabbits were the preserve of the keepers rather than the owners of the estates and they made good pocket money. As a result, they were carefully preserved and when isolated populations died out in a remote glen, maybe because of a really severe winter of deep snow, the keepers collected rabbits from other areas to restore their populations. The trade in rabbits was really important and even people on remote islands like Fair Isle shot and exported them to the London markets by boat and train, loaded into special rabbit boxes. When myxomatosis turned the British public against eating rabbit meat, a regular income for many country people dried up overnight.

Rabbits were common in the Scottish Highlands and Islands during most of my working life in bird conservation. They were a favourite prey of golden eagle, buzzard and wildcat. When we reintroduced the red kite to the Black Isle near Inverness, rabbits proved to be one of their most important foods. The number of rabbits was incredible and we could easily drive around the roads early in the morning and collect half-a-dozen road casualty rabbits to feed our young kites. Once the birds were released and spreading out over the countryside, farmers would phone me to say that a kite had arrived and was living on their farm, and they'd wonder if there was anything they could do to help. I would ask them to shoot a rabbit several times a week and put it out on an open field, so the young kite could come down and find easy food. And they did.

After the millennium, I was living in Moray where one of my best osprey study areas was located. A monitoring trip round the nests might be about 130 kilometres and in that distance I'd probably see several hundred rabbits or more. They were incredibly common and farmers' crops were often severely grazed around the edges. Outbreaks of myxomatosis regularly occurred and numbers would go down for a short time and then bounce back. Rabbits were plentiful in 2009 and that August you could smell dead rabbits in the undergrowth. But then the survivors got rabbit haemorrhagic disease (RHD), which had been spreading up from the south, either naturally or leapfrogged by human intervention, and suddenly the rabbits were all gone. They died unseen in their burrows; unlike 'myxy rabbits', which could be seen wandering around with weeping eyes.

Even now, more than a decade later, it's uncommon to see a rabbit. If I'm lucky, I may see one on a similar osprey monitoring drive, and numbers hang out in remote areas and islands. The loss of most wild rabbits in the Highlands has had a dramatic impact on wildcat, for before 2009 I would see the cats in our district while now there are none; buzzard numbers have dropped and breeding success is poor. I'm sure that the loss of rabbits has also put pressure on other wildlife, as the predators that once favoured rabbit seek out new food sources. I guess, one day, the rabbits will get over RHD as they did myxomatosis, although I hear there's an even worse form of RHD on the scene.

In the early years of this century I was a regular visitor to Andalucía when I helped with the Spanish osprey reintroduction project. Several times when at Coto Doñana National Park I went with wardens to try to see an Iberian lynx but, sadly, I was unlucky, despite their having been seen in exactly the same place not long before. One time my friend stopped and looked at the photos in his trail camera, attached to a track-side tree, and there was a photo of a male lynx strolling down the track at the same time but a day earlier. I also saw the huge efforts to rebuild the rabbit population by translocating rabbits to specially built and protected warrens. It proved very difficult and just showed that losing rabbits can be easy but restoring them very difficult.

Rabbits – here today, gone tomorrow

Restored rabbit populations would be beneficial for some of our iconic species such as wildcat and golden eagle, and I wish there were still the old keepers who had the skills to restore the rabbit to remote glens. What's really interesting, though, is that it's now frowned upon to move rabbits around our countryside to restore populations. The rabbit is now seen, by many, as an undesirable alien despite the fact it's been here for over 1,000 years, nearly as long as the brown hare, which we view very differently and which most people think is a native mammal.

# Let's have a sacred mountain

As a young, nature-loving child, I was lucky to grow up in country-side surprisingly wild in nature. I could secretly camp in hidden places in the New Forest, unknown to the foresters and keepers, and earlier, before I was ten and knew better, I collected bird's eggs, tamed young jackdaws and kept newts in my aquarium. Very few people went birdwatching, wild camping or long-distance hiking – we naturalists had no real impact on nature, but there were others who killed wildlife, like raptors or hunted otters, sometimes in large numbers.

Then in the 1950s and 1960s came the pesticide era, with its massive impact on wildlife. The way my mum used DDT on houseflies, I'm almost surprised I survived. Then came the ever-increasing mechanisation of farming with dramatic changes that finally led to the loss of the once common birds, insects and flowers of my childhood. Glorious hedgerows, farm ponds and gnarled old trees we climbed disappeared. Our food got cheaper but our enjoyment grew less.

Each new generation of my nature-loving friends accept lower experiences and expectations. It's called baseline creep, so that what we have now does not seem so bad if we compare it to the 1990s rather than to the 1960s. But there is one other change that has been massive in the second half of my life and that's the extent of leisure and recreation.

I'm fortunate to live in Moray, a beautiful county, much of which is still very rural and relatively unchanged, but if I drive south over Dava Moor I'm in the Cairngorms National Park. Is nature better looked after there? Sadly not, because of burgeoning recreational activities and increasing numbers of people. How does society look after wildlife when increasing numbers of people use the same land? The Scottish Access Laws gave everyone the right to roam (responsibly), but how does that work? The slogan 'respect wildlife' is only meaningful if people not only know what that means but how to behave.

Maybe it would be better to agree that an activity like taking dogs into nature reserves or carrying out disturbing recreation everywhere is not in the best interests of nature. On the coast in winter, most of the wader and wildfowl roosts, even the remote ones I knew when younger, are now regularly disturbed by dog walkers. I think it is time our Scottish Government and Scottish Natural Heritage completed the thinking on nature conserva-tion in the access legislation. Surely the 10 per cent or so of the countryside specially designated for nature should get a better deal from us? They should be places where nature comes first, and where we tread with a very light foot, or not at all, giving nature real respect.

The interesting thing is that countryside users often blame developers, farmers, foresters, landowners and the like for dam-aging wildlife and the countryside, and often rightly so, but rarely do they think that their activities do any damage. In essence, it's not restrictions that will solve the problem but a genuine change in our attitudes, where we truly respect nature and give it room to live and evolve. We need to make a conscious decision that we don't need to go everywhere.

On a beautiful evening in 2015, I looked across the Swiss countryside to the Matterhorn, and my friends told me that the town of Zermatt was celebrating the 150th anniversary of Edward Whymper making the first ascent of the mountain. They also said that out of respect for the mountain it would be unclimbed on that day. Other countries have sacred places for a variety of reasons. Famous mountains, like Kailash in the

Himalayas, are held in high esteem, and spiritual considerations preclude human access. It's fine to look at it and revere it from a distance, but not to climb and despoil it.

I think it would be a wonderful gift to nature if Scotland had one mountain that no one would ever climb again. I'm not spiritual, but what a way that would be to show our love of nature. I wonder which one it should be?

# Nature and the problems of tidiness

Many years ago, I was talking with a group of crofters in Sutherland and someone mentioned the word 'poaching' with regard to red deer. I loved the comment from one of the Gaelic speakers present that there was no such word in the Gaelic language! Of course, they knew the principle of 'one for the pot'.

Equally, when people talk about mess in the countryside, I'm reminded that wildlife doesn't know the word. In fact, what wildlife really doesn't like is tidiness. But tidiness has been part of our behaviour for a long time. We are encouraged to keep things tidy and not to live in a mess, and for long enough cleanliness was next to godliness in many people's minds. Fortunately for nature, some of that is starting to slip away, thank goodness.

Over my lifetime, I've seen many examples of misplaced tidiness, even on nature reserves. A tree falls over and someone immediately thinks they have to tidy it up, cut it into logs, take it home and burn the remaining brash. Well, that's not much use to nature. When I was younger and foresters were harvesting compartments of timber in their woods, it was accepted practice to cut down all dead trees and non-commercial species, so that everything looked nice and neat after the timber had been extracted. In 1979, I visited Swedish forests on a study tour of goldeneye and osprey conservation projects. In Värmland, I was delighted to see that the woodcutters had left the dead trees standing across the big sweeps of clear fell. When I asked a forester about the practice, he told me that it was to provide perches for raptors and owls, so they could kill small rodents, day or night, to prevent damage to the new young trees. I liked that. When I got home I gave talks to groups of foresters, including students at Aberdeen University, and you could see the disbelief, especially on the older ones' faces. It took several decades for the younger ones to take over. Now, dead trees are left standing to the benefit of nature.

There is more biodiversity in woods that include some standing dead trees, and even greater value when there are also fallen ones. This, though, is a difficult concept for many. I remember years ago travelling around the Black Forest with two German osprey colleagues. In a week I found only about half a dozen conifers with flat or broken tops suitable for nesting ospreys; German foresters were very proud of their silvicultural traditions and quickly removed any trees with signs of damage or disease. This tidying up was aimed at getting the maximum number of timber trees suitable for the sawmill, but also was evidence of a tidy forester. It missed the greater values of forests, but it seems to be part of human life. We just like tidying up. A new angle on this is wood chipping as a method of getting rid of branches and small trees. This is acceptable in urban situations but not in the wider countryside, where piles of brash are such important habitats for wildlife, finally rotting down to the benefit of the myriad of small organisms. I guess wood chipping shows that you are doing something and that you still have that 'tidy' gene. My advice is: let it go.

Cutting lawns and roadsides is a never-ending way of promoting tidiness but at what a cost to flowers and insects. The verge outside our house is now left uncut when the council worker with his tractor flail comes by, as he recognises that we like our verge with its wild flowers. But think of big lawns – and in my area there are some very expansive ones. Why not let half go to flower meadow? I didn't think to cut our lawn for a while this summer and soon it was covered in white clover flowers. I eventually went to get the mower but realised that the whole lawn was covered in bumblebees, and they took precedence over tidiness. Sometimes an anxious person whose garden includes thistles and nettles asks me how they should respond to criticism. My advice is to remind their critics that these plants are important for butterflies and bees, and that nettles are a special food for caterpillars. Be proud, not ashamed!

Mud is another problem area. Wildlife loves it, but we don't seem to like muddy boots. Sometimes when I'm in forests, I'll come across a track used by massive machines to fell and extract timber. The track is full of big holes and scars, and most often they get a resurface. But how much better it is when they are left alone! Then, in the following spring, they are full of water and of life. How quickly the frogs find them for spawning; all sorts of invertebrates dive in, dragonflies dance over them and all those birds that use mud in their nest-building have a ready supply. It's much the same with cattle when they are ploutering around the edges of ponds and rivers. Firstly, they make a plentiful supply of nest-building materials for swallows and house martins; then there are micro-pools in the footprints, as well as a haven for small life in the mix of mud, urine and dung.

Now, too often, we exclude cattle from water margins for a variety of reasons and I'm sure that's not in the best interests of nature. Cattle used to visit a lochan on a farm near my old home, and they created the most wonderful muddy place for birds. The lapwings and redshanks took their young there to feed and for several years it was the haunt for a pair of very rare green sand-pipers. An agri-environment programme came on the scene and the farmer was advised that he would get a special payment if he protected the lochan with a fence. In no time at all, the vegetation grew and became rank, the muddy edge was lost and the breeding waders were gone. It was a real loss of biodiversity in the guise of progress and it's a mistake that has been made time and time again. If the lapwings could talk, they would tell us to stop tidying up the countryside. And the rest of nature would agree.

# Bringing back the beaver

In 2017, I visited an osprey nest in Strathspey and ringed the single chick, the first young there after a gap of eight years. The eyrie was atop an ancient Scots pine growing in a bog. On earlier visits I had needed to jump ditches and wade through swampy areas to reach the tree, but now everywhere was dry and the patches of open water all vegetated over.

This had been such a special forest bog where the ospreys had nesting teal and very rare green sandpipers as neighbours. This forest has every sort of conservation designation possible but it has lost a lot of its value through the uncontrolled growth of excess vegetation, due to lack of big herbivores, originally auroch, moose and beaver. It was clear to me that the immediate remedy for such a special area would be the return of beavers. In a few years, their activities would bring these forest bogs and pools back to life, as well as opening up and rewetting the other low-lying parts of the forest. They would slow down the small river and create even more wetlands. I firmly believe that the Scottish government's refusal to allow beavers back in all these wet woodlands is seriously detrimental to wildlife conservation and our international obligations.

In 2019, the centenary year of the Forestry Commission in England, I addressed their annual conference at the University of Exeter and gave my views on where they should be heading ecologically. One of the delegates was Professor Richard Brazier, whose team had carried out detailed scientific studies on beavers that had been placed in a wet woodland reserve in north Devon. Their results were very impressive and showed how the beavers had changed the ecosystem by building a chain of dams that slowed down the small river coming from the adjacent farmland. Water flows had been ameliorated as water was held in the dams, and sediments and chemicals had been deposited within the site. The water coming out of the wood was much purified and the wildlife benefits for other species outstanding. In fact, the fourteen dams held 1,000 cubic metres of water and had captured 100 tonnes of silt. I remember walking there nearly ten years before with Derek Gow, who is the pioneer and champion of the return of the beaver as a water engineer and ecological improver. Just about everything we talked about then has been proved by these studies and others.

Similar results have been obtained by PhD researchers on beavers and their impacts in the River Tay catchment in Scotland, yet we are still experiencing resistance to the return of the species to other areas of the UK. It saddens me greatly that board members and staff of the then newly created Scottish Natural Heritage discussed the need to reintroduce the beaver in the early 1990s and here we are, twenty-five years later, still dithering about full-scale recovery, although they are now legally protected. Then, our interest was very much about the ecological and wildlife benefits they would bring. Now, though, with an ever-increasing recognition that we must restore natural processes for the benefit of people as well as wildlife, we have the evidence that beavers can help alleviate downstream flooding, maintain water in streams in times of drought, slow down the run-off loss of soils and help prevent agricultural chemicals from pouring down rivers and into lochs, estuaries and the sea. You would think it's a no-brainer. Sadly, that's not how it works.

Forty years ago, I saw my first beavers in the wild when staying on a farm in Jämtland in Sweden. My host, Erik, was a hunter and a farmer who also worked in the local town; his family farm was in beautiful countryside with ospreys, goldeneye ducks and cranes breeding in the bogs, while in the forests lived elk and beavers. I remember thinking that it was as Scotland should be. One evening, I walked to the sluggish river that ran nearby and, after a mosquito-tormented stalk, saw my first beaver; it sensed my presence, though, and with a slap of its tail was gone. I sat down on a jumble of beaver-felled birch trees but my wait for further sightings was in vain. I asked Erik what he thought about the beavers and the birch trees felled by them lying across his track. His reply was sensible. 'I wait until winter and then drive down with my tractor and trailer and log up those trees – they are nicely seasoned and ready for my log store. And sometimes I hunt one. Would you like beaver for supper tomorrow? I'll get some out of the deep freeze.' I thought it tasted good, nicely braised, somewhere between brown hare and roe. I liked the matter-of-fact way in which he lived with the beavers and also recognised their value in the wetland ecosystem.

Initially, sport fishermen on salmon and trout rivers were doubtful about beavers, with some even thinking that they ate fish. Much of that misunderstanding has gone, though, and there is recognition that beavers and salmon have lived together for aeons. Dramatic social changes can happen; the fishermen in the Cévennes mountains of France used to break down beaver dams to protect their fish until, on a visit during a summer of severe drought, they found all their young fish sheltering in the beaver ponds. The dam destruction ceased.

Beavers need pragmatic management, but it is essential to listen to and understand complaints. When beavers raid crops and create holes in farm fields, it's usually due to the cultivation being far too close to rivers. From now on, rivers running through cultivated farmland should always have a band of natural vegetation lining the banks to create a barrier to agricultural run-off. Farming chemicals and fertilisers leaching off soils are a serious problem in rivers, estuaries and the open sea. These barriers will also reduce problems with beavers. It's important to remember that the great bulk of farmers will never see a beaver near their land and the benefits of beavers to our ecosystems outweigh any damage.

I suppose there is reluctance to have beavers return to Britain because we killed them all long ago – not because they were a pest but because their fur and oil were so valuable. But when I think of my visits to Sweden, Germany, the Netherlands and Belgium, I just don't understand it. There are so many advantages, some big, some small, in having beavers in a river. I remember a Belgian friend explaining the thrill he experienced when the first pair of black storks arrived to breed on one of his beaver streams in the Ardennes. Then, years later, a beaver researcher found a black stork image on his trail cameras deployed at a beaver site in the Highlands.

The beaver is something special for restoring biodiversity. That's why I believe that it's crucial for all of us to learn to accept that, although some species may at times cause some of us problems, we should remember the myriad of species and actions of the natural world that allow us to farm and fish, grow crops and trees, have fresh water and breathe fresh air. We, like the beavers, are part of the great ecosystem we call the Earth. The beaver should return with our blessing and gratitude.

# The ecology of changing
# goose numbers

Whereas in my lifetime many species of birds have declined or even, like grey partridge, near enough disappeared, geese have done very well in the last fifty years. The first geese I really knew, as a young birdwatcher in Hampshire, were the flocks of brent geese that migrated to our estuaries for the winter from Siberia. When I was sixteen, I volunteered to collect their droppings on the mudflats of Langstone Harbour for a Nature Conservancy scientist, who was researching the food of the brents. Once a month we would launch a small boat, carried there on the roof of his Land Rover, into the harbour on the falling tide. I would be dropped on a big mud bank, his girlfriend on the next, while he would head for the furthest. My task was to collect into big bags as many as possible of the greenish goose droppings, with a promise that I would be collected on the rising tide. It was great fun, in the days before institutional Health and Safety, although I had learnt about risk as a boy when swimming in tidal estuaries.

We knew the brent geese as very shy and scarce birds. Hunting them with shotguns or punt guns, by wildfowlers, was stopped in 1954 to safeguard the species. It responded rapidly and the UK wintering population grew from 15,000 to 300,000 in thirty years, with the bird completely changing its habits. Instead of being difficult to approach, they would now readily feed along the coasts within sight of people, and even on the grass of sports fields and parks nearby.

When I came north to live in Scotland, greylag and pink-footed geese were my regular species. They have both increased during my lifetime, but quite differently. I first saw them on migration at

Fair Isle in 1959, where they were eagerly hunted by the islanders who loved eating goose as a change in their spartan diet. In fact, in the 1960s most people could pluck, gut and cook a goose, while now, if you offered people a wild goose for their dinner, very few would know what to do with it or even wish to eat it. It is an excellent food and far better for you than a pizza or a ready meal.

Breeding greylags in Scotland were restricted to small summer-protected populations in the Uists, Wester Ross and Sutherland. They then started to increase in the 1970s and we, in the Highland Ringing Group, caught and ringed some when they moulted. Many were translocated by wildfowlers to southern areas of Britain. Nowadays, descendants of those wild geese, as well as the feral greylags, are booming. Locals no longer hunt them for food in winter as they used to, so the population continues to grow, but I guess their numbers may start to be checked by the restored white-tailed eagles, which have started to hunt the goslings successfully. With global warming, more of the wintering greylags stay at home in Iceland or stop over in Shetland and Orkney, where most islanders no longer yearn for roast goose.

If the numbers of Icelandic greylag geese migrating to Britain in autumn has declined, the opposite is true of pink-footed geese, which have gone up from 50,000 in 1960 to about half a million now. This massive increase is due in part to declining hunting, but mainly to their benefiting from the intensification of agriculture. Large fields of newly cut barley and wheat in the autumn are eagerly sought, before they move later to potato and carrot fields after harvesting. Finally, before going home, they graze on winter cereals and other crops in the spring. All of the crops are liberally supplied with artificial fertilisers, which make them even more attractive to the geese. The farmers complain about the numbers, but geese can be legitimately shot in autumn and winter, so I guess it's too much bother to shoot a bird that no one wants to eat.

In 1994, I went with Sir John Lister-Kaye and Dr Greg Mudge on a Scottish Natural Heritage study tour to investigate the hunting of Canada geese in Chesapeake Bay, on the east coast of the US. In order to make some extra income, the hunters and farmers we met shot a few geese each on the dawn flights, then retired to a local café with their friends to chat while, next door, the geese were plucked, gutted and vacuum packed. A small charge was made to the hunters and the pluckers sold the feathers. We thought it a good model for Scotland but it's never really been taken up. What works for one country doesn't always work for another.

It's all about numbers. One morning in October 2016 I counted 52,000 pink-footed geese at Findhorn Bay; they were on passage from Iceland. As the sun rose and illuminated the great flock of birds out on the sands, they shone brown and grey, in fact nearly golden. In a crescendo of calling, they rose in great skeins, heading off to feed or fly further south. The spectacle of very large numbers makes a flock of 200 seem tame. The single snow goose with them, a vagrant from North America, was very interesting to us birdwatchers, however, despite the fact that three million live over there.

What's the problem with very large numbers of geese? There's damage to agriculture, fouling on parks and golf courses and, in some places, danger to aircraft. But what about the ecological impacts? These came home to me again when I visited Ny-Ålesund on Svalbard in 1994, and talked with scientists studying barnacle geese. Many of those barnacles winter in the Solway Firth, where the population has increased from 1,500 in 1960 to 40,000. As we landed from our wildlife cruise boat and walked up over the island, the vegetation was like a golf course, cropped short by the geese, and it made me think of overgrazing by red deer in Scotland. Then we noticed that many of the geese were nesting in small wooden shelters. The goose researchers said it was to save the eggs from predation by skuas. That year there was an even bigger problem, they complained: an Arctic fox had turned up and started eating the eggs. They had to catch it and transport it far inland by snow scooter. Sadly, their minds were solely on goose research, rather than ecology or the overgrazing of Arctic plants.

Earlier, in July 1988, a team of us went on a month-long Wildfowl Trust expedition to north-east Greenland to catch and ring geese. Pink-footed and barnacle geese bred on and around the great Hold with Hope peninsula, and our plan was to catch as many moulting geese and their young as possible on the numerous small lakes. It was a magical place, called by some the 'Riviera of the Arctic', with beautiful flowers, nesting waders, musk ox and even butterflies. Lemming numbers were at a low so predators like skuas, foxes and polar wolves were hungry. They were concentrating on birds' eggs, young birds and moulting adult geese. In consequence, the geese could not wander far from the water because they would be ambushed by the mammal predators, and so had completely overgrazed the vegetation within a hundred metres or so of the water's edge. This had removed the vegetative cover favoured by birds such as red-throated divers and grey phalaropes, which like to hide their nests close to the water's edge.

It was clear to me that the conditions on the wintering grounds – through reductions in predators, including man, and superabundant winter food – were negatively impacting the Arctic breeding grounds. So when I see huge numbers of geese of heading north in the spring, I fear for the nesting birds and the summer flowers of the Arctic. The breeding success of some geese could be curtailed in future by our increasing white-tailed eagle population, and, of course, we could try to eat more of them. Goose management will be a hot topic for decades to come.

# Looking at a footprint and thinking, 'Bear!'

Staring at the huge footprint of a brown bear in the muddy track set me thinking. We had walked through the morning up a woodland track and reached the higher forest in the Low Tatra National Park in Slovakia. Our guide, Robin Rigg, who lived with his wife and children in the village on the other side of the mountain, told us about the large carnivores in his home patch. Then there was another bear pad mark and, a little further on, four hunters, eating a superb goulash made from a red deer they had hunted the previous evening, told us of a big bear they had seen earlier that morning. To me, that makes the forest alive. By the way, the chief hunter told me exactly how to make the best goulash. 'Make certain the bacon in the first step is completely browned and absorbed in the olive oil.' Now, when I make the dish at home, I always think of that forest hut in Slovakia in October 2008.

More bear signs were obvious as we hiked on over the ridge, but we failed to find a lynx pad mark and the possible wolf print was more likely that of a forester's dog. Down through the wooded slopes to Robin's village we walked, talking of large carnivores, their places in nature and their relationship with people. Earlier in the day we'd seen Robin's work, with the Slovak Wildlife Society, designing more effective electric fencing to deter bears from raiding hives to eat bees, larva and honey. Yet crossing the river and walking through the little camping area to our car, we learned that the tracks of wolf, bear and lynx could all be seen this close to people.

For me, walking through forests in the presence of predators makes the experience special. Compare this with walks at home, where winter snows no longer show the passing of a lynx or the trail of a wolf pack. What a loss, what a diminution of the predator-prey hierarchy.

The Low Tatra National Park covers about 2,000 square kilometres and the population estimates then were 100 to 150 brown bears, four or five packs of wolves with maybe thirty individuals in total, and about thirty to forty lynx. They were also present in the High Tatra, the Slovak Paradise National Park, and the Karst and Poloniny National Parks. The national totals were estimated at 600 to 800 brown bears, 400 lynx and 150 to 350 wolves. All these large mammals were part of the Carpathian population, with the largest numbers being in Romania.

Robin told us of the work of the Slovak Wildlife Society in trying to reconcile the conservation of large carnivores with their co-existence with humans. The increasing interest in them, and their eco-tourism value, contrasted with the views of those Slovaks who were scared of, or simply disliked, them. Attacks by bears were very rare but the few that did occur were high profile. The least well known was the lynx, which was a secret presence living in the forests and rarely seen. They were protected, although we heard that a licence had been granted to kill some lynx in the High Tatra National Park because of a complaint about predation of the local subspecies of the chamois.

As we walked home we watched a forester's horse dragging logs, and below in the valley were country people, townspeople and tourists all going about their business with no thought of the lynx living in the woodlands, never seen and never heard by any but a tiny number of people. How easily this animal can live in our midst. Once again, I was disheartened by the fact that we have not yet restored the lynx to Scotland. Slovak lynxes were used to restore the species in Switzerland and Slovenia and, when asked, one of our hosts said he was sure that Slovakia could provide donor animals for Scotland. We should take him up on his offer and reintroduce this magnificent cat to our country. Ecologically we have room, we have ideal habitats and a plentiful supply of wild prey, and the lynx could play an important role in controlling and changing the behaviour of our middle-guild predators, especially fox and badger. We just need to resolve the social and political objections to an important advance in nature conservation, and at the end of the day one interest group should not be able to hold up the restoration of a key species in the countryside.

# Chance and the Wilson's warbler

In 2014, an old friend, Tony Marr, asked me to come over to Port of Ness, the most northerly village in the Outer Hebrides, to open the new bird hide at Loch Stiapabhat in the north end of the island of Lewis. Tony and I both started birding on the south coast, he in Sussex and me in Hampshire. He now lives at Cley in North Norfolk but to get some peace when birding he chose to buy a cottage at Port of Ness. There he can birdwatch every day and when he finds rare birds he can watch them without a large gathering of twitchers. I said I'd come back one autumn and have a few days looking for rare birds with him.

On 15th October 2017, we were out early on a most beautiful clear, sunny morning, with all the mountains of Wester Ross and Sutherland showing clearly forty miles across the Minch. At the Butt of Lewis lighthouse we saw a lovely young merlin, possibly a migrant from Iceland, mobbing a hen harrier. We checked various gardens for migrants but drew a blank, and a careful search of a big flock of golden plovers found no stray American waders. After a visit to the bird hide, it was time for lunch at his house.

Tony and I have so many old mutual friends that our lunch became extended with tales of old times and favourite stories. Suddenly it was 2p.m. and 'We're here to bird, not to talk!' so we got our binoculars and coats and headed out again. First stop was next door's excellent wooded garden – and ten minutes later we were watching a Wilson's warbler, a small and beautiful North American warbler, brilliant yellow with a tiny black crown. We got the briefest of views before it dived back into the little wood. Twenty-five minutes later, we got another good but brief view to confirm our identification. This was a mega-rarity, being the first for Scotland, second for Britain and third for Britain and Ireland combined.

Of course, it is Tony's dedication in birding every day during the migration seasons at the Butt of Lewis that gives him the excitement of finding rare birds and witnessing the annual migrations. But it's also chance. If we had not regaled each other with stories of old friends, we might have visited the garden ten minutes earlier and missed the warbler, and if we had talked too long we might have arrived too late. And then, of course, you need to be able to identify a species you've never seen before in Britain.

I headed home the next morning after a brief but brilliant birding trip, with the icing on the cake being a magic little Wilson's warbler all the way from the States. It had been great fun with great company. Tony's day would be taken up with hosting birders from around the UK, keen to see a new bird for their Scottish and British life lists. I hoped it would still be there. I later learned that it stayed three days and was seen by many birders from as far away as southern England.

*Postscript*: Alexander Wilson was born in Paisley in 1766 and was the first ornithologist to describe the species. That was in 1811, when he was carrying out fieldwork throughout North America between 1808 and 1814. He illustrated 268 species of birds for his epic publication *American Ornithology*, twenty-six of which were new to science.

# The salmon and the bear

In Moray, the River Findhorn rushes to the sea through sandstone gorges and mature forests. It's a beautiful and turbulent river, which suddenly opens out into an enclosed estuary called Findhorn Bay, a favoured haunt of waders and wildfowl, where ospreys in summer catch flounders in the shallow waters.

It's one of Scotland's famous salmon-fishing rivers but nowadays the numbers of fish are so poor that anglers have to put them back in the river until after mid-May. It's a statutory catch-and-release policy to try to restore the species, but it's not always been like that. Even I remember the rod fishermen catching large numbers of fish as the salmon headed up the river to spawn, while out on the coast the net-fishing stations were kept busy taking in large hauls. Boxed in ice, they were sent on the night train to Billingsgate fish market in London, a taste of the wild Highlands for city palates.

When I birded the coasts of the Moray Firth in the 1960s and '70s, I sometimes stopped and chatted with the salmon fishermen at their ancient bothies on Culbin Bar or Whiteness Head, and watched them harvest the king of fish. The tall nets stretched out to sea on long poles and worked as a trap for the salmon migrating along the coasts to their natal rivers.

On one occasion I called by the salmon bothy at the mouth of the River Conon, near Dingwall. The manager, Mr Tuckwell, was an old friend with an interest in birds, and I was on my way up the riverbank to check on a particularly rare bird: the diminutive Temminck's stint, nesting in a muddy field. It was one of the very few places in Scotland where it nested, far from its normal breeding grounds in northern Scandinavia. It was a sunny evening, and Mr Tuckwell told me to call by on my way back for a treat.

I remember that evening not for the stints, but for the supper. A big fresh-run salmon had been gutted, a half pound of butter and a shake of salt placed inside the cavity, the fish wrapped in a thick covering of wet newspaper and then buried in the hot stones of a fire on the riverbank. When I returned, Mr Tuckwell raked off the stones, broke open the package and, with baked tatties, the fishing crew and I enjoyed the most delicious handfuls of warm salmon.

The return of the salmon from the open ocean to freshwater rivers has been taking place for millions of years. It's quite extraordinary how these fish, hatched in the headwaters of our Scottish rivers, set off downstream and out into the seas. After a few years of feeding, they return as large and beautiful silver fish, seeking out their ancestral homes. Fighting their way upstream, the females lay their eggs to be fertilised by the males as the pair lie side by side in the gravels of the tributaries, often exactly where they were hatched. After spawning, the salmon swim down river, many of them dying, washed up on the river shingle bars. It's the most wonderful example of a natural circle: nutrients flow down the river and out to sea, and the migratory salmon bring some of them back ashore.

Think, though, what those annual cycles were like, say, 5,000 years ago in Scotland. Salmon numbers would have been huge, if we're to judge by the big salmon runs in Norway, Russia and Alaska today. The salmon themselves must been crucial to many species' food chains. As they entered the estuaries and river mouths, they were grabbed and eaten by seals, bottle-nosed dolphins and killer whales. Forging up the rivers to spawn in the headwaters, they had waiting for them a whole range of creatures. White-tailed eagles scooped them out of the shallows when they were laying their eggs in the gravels. Wolves would crash into the rivers and rush after them; they might eat them on the riverbank or carry them away to their pups in dens in the forests or mountains. The ancient brown bears of Scotland would have been expert catchers of salmon, a scene we can conjure up still from watching nature programmes about their Alaskan counterparts.

Bears and salmon belong together in many parts of the world, often featuring in superb woodcarvings by the native peoples of North America and Asia, which I've seen for myself on the coast of Washington state and the northern Japanese island of Hokkaido. The bears would drag the great fish ashore but didn't necessarily eat them all, meaning that there was plenty left for others. Ravens, crows, kites and buzzards, red foxes and badgers were just the start of a hungry queue for salmon. Some fish may have been carried hundreds of yards into the forest, where their remains would fertilise the growth of plants and young trees. The salmon's return to the land was important for the whole ecology of river catchments.

Next, of course, early man jumped in and took salmon with his spears and traps. Now, the salmon is rare because of man-made problems at sea, ranging from terrifyingly efficient commercial fisheries to rising temperatures that negatively affect the small fish on which they feed at sea. Now, too, there's very little recycling from the oceans and the headwaters are impoverished. Salmon are still eaten by humans in large quantities, but nearly all of them come from marine fish farms, with the residues going into sewer systems rather than onto the land as it did long ago. All in all, we're watching the loss of a very special ecosystem driver.

# Our place on the planet

It's always important to remember that we are a species in the natural world and not outside it, although that's often difficult to believe. It's fascinating to think that at one stage, our ancestors, although apex predators, were regularly killed by other species. Now we seem to be outside looking in, instead of continuing to be part of the natural world. Lots of changes have taken place and there have been many times when our forebears have reached tipping points. One of our ancient ancestors, the Neanderthals (for most of us in Europe have about 3 or 4 per cent of their DNA) had a relatively light impact on species or habitats; they certainly learned how to kill big animals by making spears with sharp flintheads and traps.

Early man made many advances, numbers increased and they learnt to work together in tribes; they killed big animals but were still subject to being killed and eaten by big predators such as the sabre-toothed cat. They learnt to control fire and use it to keep themselves warm, to cook and to keep away dangerous animals after dark. At a camp night at my daughter's primary school, parents sat around the fire, chatting and telling stories while the children played. It was no different to what our ancient ancestors did around those first fires, which are thought to be the reason humans talk so much.

As our species started to colonise the world from Africa, many of the mega-fauna were exterminated, but the impact on most of nature was still relatively small. In Europe, our ancestors overtook and pushed aside the Neanderthals and hunted woolly mammoth, rhinoceros and elephant to extinction. Once cattle, sheep, goats and horses had been successfully domesticated, about ten millennia or more ago, and crop growing had become efficient, humans were able to really expand and clear natural areas for grazing lands through burning. Yet they were still mammals in the system, even if, increasingly, they were the dominant one.

The builders of magical places like Maeshowe in Orkney probably chose the islands for their homes and living places because of the lack of predatory mammals compared to mainland Scotland. Early man was certainly capable of dealing with these threats and soon colonised the mainland of the British Isles, but even so, brown bear survived until 1,000 years ago and the wolf was not exterminated until the mid-eighteenth century. The pace of change had already sped up and in the last several centuries humans have had dramatic effects on nature throughout the world.

These effects have come about by direct killing, by destroying habitats to build the infrastructure of modern man and by many other indirect impacts, leading to more than half a century of intense change through the use of man-made chemicals and many forms of pollution as the human population has grown and grown. Most of our impacts on nature have been negative and extremely damaging and, most worryingly, still continue to be. In the last hundred years or more we have started to recognise our responsibilities by creating nature reserves, protected areas, national parks and wildlife laws. And there are many wonderful people devoting their life's work to reversing the losses and creating a better world.

But the real issue is that although biodiversity conservation and the protection of the Earth's ecosystems are essential for a safe future for us and nature, they receive neither real political clout nor money. Way back in 1991, while on the board of Scottish Natural Heritage, I wrote a couple of discussion papers in which I pointed out the shortcomings in biodiversity survival. Why did we spend far more money per year on cosmetics (for both men and women) and chocolates than on Scotland's biosphere, without which we had no safe future? And if we looked further, why did we spend more on works of art than on nature? I guess the answer is because humans can make a profit out of the former. And then look at where governments spend the big money. I always felt frustrated with my wildlife peers for failing to tell our government that we could not secure the long-term future of Scotland's biodiversity without a major increase in funding and standing. That always rattled me and it came back to me locally, many years later, when the UK government took the decision to scrap the new Nimrod aircraft – wasting our nation about £3.5 billion, it was estimated. In the same era, it was severely cutting the nation's ecological agencies, which spent a tiny fraction of this amount.

We have reached a time in the history of our planet when many of the everyday problems of nations will pale into insignificance unless we address global warming, chemical pollution and the over-exploitation of the Earth's nature and natural processes.

# Right trees, wrong places

In the 1970s and '80s, a lot of my time and energy while working for the RSPB was taken up with arguments not just about birds, but about trees. It was the time of the 'great flow country' controversy in northern Scotland, when huge tracts of virgin peat lands were being ploughed and planted with Sitka spruce and lodgepole pine. These are non-native trees, imports from North America, and we quickly learnt that most of the planting was driven by the desire to earn tax advantages for very wealthy people, and organised by determined timber companies. Great swathes of lodgepole pine were also being devoured by the caterpillars of the pine beauty moth, with affected plantations sprayed from the air with chemicals. It was clearly an ecological mismatch to plant two exotics across such vast acreages and on such poor soils.

An international conference on ospreys and bald eagles was held in Montreal in 1981 and I got the chance to present a paper on ospreys in Scotland and be involved in the debates. I also wanted to take the opportunity to see Sitka spruce, Douglas fir and lodgepole pine growing in their native North American habitats. It would put me ahead of the game in discussions and arguments with Scottish foresters.

A research biologist at the Olympic National Park based in Port Angeles, across Puget Sound from Seattle, offered to host me for a short visit. On my first morning, Bruce picked me up from the research bunkhouse and drove me up the steeply winding mountain road to Hurricane Ridge, where we burst out of the sea fog to see glorious mountains and forests, with the stunning vista of Mount Baker in the distance and the fog now far below us, filling the valleys. We hiked upwards, talking about the park's projects on soil erosion, stopping to look at the local flora and the resident shaggy white mountain goats. The latter posed a real dilemma for the National Park: they were non-native but were the most commonly seen large mammals for visitors. I saw lots of new bird species – varied thrush, Steller's jay, kinglet and pine siskin – and we talked of cougars, which lived in the area but never showed themselves. I liked to hope, though.

Later in the week, I set aside a whole day to drive to the Hoh River valley on the Pacific coast. I passed through Forks, a small town built around logging and timber businesses, and by midday was at the western entrance to the National Park, home to some of the finest untouched forests of the Northwest. Walking up the track that leads to Mount Olympus, I entered into a wood of immense trees. Like the columns of a mighty cathedral, the Douglas firs, western hemlocks and Sitka spruces stretched upwards to the sky. Some reached almost 100 metres, their bases almost five metres across. In places these massive giants, many more than 300 years old, were in straight lines, forming what locals call a colonnade. Young trees had started to grow 200 years or more ago along the top of a giant old or dying tree that had crashed down through the forest to create a long thin glimpse of the sky. This had provided enough new light for young trees to climb upwards and the rotted mother trees were ideal for growth, safe from the nibbling of deer. Many of the trees were festooned with vine maples, hanging with mosses and an understorey of salmon berry, with alders near the river. I saw black-tailed deer and Douglas squirrels, while in wet sand near the river were the pug marks of a cougar, five or six inches across.

It was a lovely day and I stopped on a big bank overlooking the Hoh River to eat my sandwiches, with Mount Tom in the distance. I was learning the calls of chickadees, a lookalike of our coal tits, as well as North American warblers and thrushes, all of them new to me. I tried to get them to come closer by squeaking through my fingers, a trick I used at home to get skulking birds to come out of the bushes and allow me to identify them. It's a tried and tested method and soon I had black-capped chickadees, golden-crowned kinglets and gray jays coming down through the vine maples to me. It was fun: they were so close. Suddenly, though, I had the feeling that something was behind me and the hairs on the back of my neck stood up. I turned around, slowly, hoping it was not a black bear. Five metres from me was a very inquisitive coyote. I managed to get a quick photo before it shot off, possibly more surprised than I was.

While sitting in the sun I thought about one of the most enigmatic seabirds in the world, which lived in these great forests in spring and summer. The old loggers called the bird the 'fog lark', for they saw and heard it calling in the mist above them as they brought the great trees crashing to the ground with axes and saws. Amazingly, though, it was not until 1974 that a tree surgeon, climbing a monster Douglas fir in northern California, came across an odd potato-shaped bird sitting on a nest at 50 metres. The nest was just a small hollow in the moss growing on a broad branch and contained a single egg. He had inadvertently found the nesting place of the marbled murrelet, a small seabird, and the last bird in North America to have its nesting habitat revealed.

My journey continued. I jumped on another plane and got off at Missoula. A friend of a friend took me on a long, winding track high into the Bitterroot Wilderness, where the mountains of Montana abut those of Idaho. I stayed at the Lost Horse Creek ranger station, where the few staff checked hunters' permits and kept watch for forest fires. Next morning, another Bruce took me out on a trek to the watershed at 2,300 metres, where he left me to continue on foot along the ridge. It was another beautiful day and I saw many birds, including golden eagles, ravens, pine grosbeaks and cedar waxwings, as well as the most amazing tall lodgepole pines growing with Engelmann spruce and, lower down, ponderosa pine. The lodgepoles were slender trees reaching high into the sky, and so named because they are the favoured tree of the Native Americans, who cut the main poles to build their lodges.

Next morning, I awoke to a northerly wind and snow. Soon the tracks would be closed for the winter, and it was time for me to leave. I took with me a completely new appreciation of the three great trees of the American Northwest.

At home, I was now able to talk from experience when discussing these exotic tree species growing in Scotland. Most foresters had never seen them in their native lands. A Sitka spruce or a Douglas fir is still only young at 100 years old: to become a true giant it needs another century or more. The trees being planted in Scotland were all likely to be harvested by the time they were fifty. This was a monoculture completely different from the Hoh River valley with its outstanding mix of trees, shrubs, plants and mosses. The exotics would never reach their potential height and slender beauty on our poor, exposed soils. To make matters worse, much of the lodgepole pine seed used for planting in Scotland had been gathered by locals in the Pacific coastal areas, where it was easy to scoop floating seed from calm inlets. These trees near the sea are bushy, many stemmed and pretty useless for timber. And that's what we found in Scotland.

As a naturalist working for the RSPB, it was a stressful time trying to protect the unique peatlands of Sutherland and Caithness, the home of greenshanks, golden plovers, red-throated divers and scoters, with sublime vistas stretching to the horizon. Finally, we managed to get public opinion to start to turn against the use of public funds to destroy such important wildlife areas in order to plant the trees. I vividly remember organising a helicopter tour of the area when Magnus Magnusson, then RSPB President, gave a brilliant exposé for TV news of the damage being done. Looking down from above, we saw that the miles and miles of plough lines through the deep peats were filled with water; they shone in the sun, an appalling onslaught on nature. We found the scene truly shocking.

Slowly but surely, though, opinions changed until, nearly overnight, tax benefits for wealthy clients were stopped and the worst of the ploughing ceased. Society started to understand the importance of peatlands for storing carbon. Decades later, though, we can see the long-term results of this short-term thinking: wildlife populations missing, whole plantations blown down by the wind, local roads damaged by timber lorries and no sign of the bonanza of local sawmill jobs that was promised at the time.

I hope the lessons have been learned. There is no room for huge monoculture plantations. We must vary the species planted and favour native trees and shrubs to restore the uplands, aim for a holistic approach and – quite simply – never plant the wrong trees in the wrong places.

# Orcas and seals

My first experience of killer whales, or orcas, was in October 1961 when we were landing on the island of Shillay in the Outer Hebrides. I was a very junior member of a group of four scientists from the Nature Conservancy in Edinburgh, studying grey seal ecology. We were taken to the Hebrides on a minesweeper, captained by the unforgettably named Lt Dickie Dumas, from the naval base at Inverewe, and we anchored for the night in the lee of the neighbouring island of Pabbay. Across the water we could hear the roaring of red deer stags.

The next morning, we moved across the sound to anchor about 300 metres from Shillay, where we were going to camp; the wooden tender was lowered into the water by the crew and we started to unload our supplies to the island's sandy beach. I jumped ashore on the first trip and started to carry our stores above the tideline. The tender continued to go back and fore to the boat, when suddenly work stopped, amid a flurry of excited shouting, because a small pod of killer whales was swimming between us and them as they reloaded the tender. That was enough to put the crew in fear and it was nearly half an hour before the all-clear was given, although the orcas must have been a long way away by then.

We had an exciting stay at Shillay studying the breeding seals and their pups. Early one morning, as we dipped our bucket into the freshwater well, a seal popped its head above the surface and for a moment held our gaze. Our Africa-seasoned leader, though, said he'd once lived off zebra pee for a week, so one seal's would do no harm to our porridge and cups of tea. The Royal Navy took us then to North Rona, an amazing experience: we lived and worked among a colony of over 2,000 breeding grey seals and their pups. I was lucky to return to this colony in 1962 but that time I saw no orcas.

When I lived on Fair Isle, I never saw any orcas, for they were very rare, although I do remember a Norwegian whaler tying up at the island pier in North Haven to cut up a freshly killed lesser rorqual. Our cook scrounged some whale meat but I guess it is an acquired taste, as none of us found it palatable. Norwegian whalers were still active in Scottish waters at that time, but the onslaught on whales in our seas stopped in the 1960s.

At Fair Isle, grey seals bred on difficult-to-access beaches below the great cliffs or in caves, and I remember the excitement of climbing down the cliffs to hidden beaches to see the young pups with their mothers. At that time the islanders still hunted grey seals, and they would go to the beaches once the pups had moulted from the white fur into the beautiful, sleek, blotched blue/grey coats before heading off to sea. The islanders killed them and sent the salted skins off to a fur business in mainland Scotland, which made sealskin waistcoats, sporrans and the like. There was even a brief time when the younger white-furred pups were killed to make imitation baby seals for sale to tourists. Unsurprisingly, this quickly came to an end, and the very idea of killing seals became unacceptable and the human use of seals in Scotland was over.

The seal population throughout Scotland started to increase and fishermen complained about their numbers and their impacts on commercial fish stocks. 'Your fish and chip suppers would be cheaper if it weren't for the seals killing so many cod and haddock!' was a popular cry by fishermen. There were demands for seals – especially the larger grey seal – to be killed and the population greatly reduced, and seals were the subject of endless reports, committees, action plans and great controversy. When I was with Scottish Natural Heritage in the mid-1990s, another management plan came forward from the research branch, and I queried why there was no mention of orcas, a natural predator of Scotland's seals. My comments were pretty much dismissed, but I knew something important was being overlooked.

Fast forward another ten years and, suddenly, people visiting remote grey seal colonies were seeing orcas. A friend told me of an incredibly exciting and bloody attack by orcas on the grey seals resting at the Flannan Isles, way west of the Hebrides. From the cliff top, he saw individual orcas swimming into gullies and flushing grey seals out to deeper water, where two were killed.

Orca numbers continued to recover and they were seen more regularly at sites around our coasts. The chance of seeing orcas visiting places like Fair Isle, Sumburgh Head and the Pentland Firth became a reality. There was no doubt that some pods of killer whales were regularly visiting the same seal colonies and haul-outs to kill and eat seals: these places were back on their mental maps, just as in ancient times. Some even specialised in eating flocks of moulting eider ducks by surprise underwater attacks.

A few years back I was amazed to hear the Fair Isle warden recount the almost-unbelievable arrival of a pod of orcas in the sheltered North Haven harbour, close to the bird observatory. The orcas killed one grey seal and were eating it close to the pier while the bull tried to bow-wave another seal off a rock close to the shore. Only the shallow depth of the water saved the seal. With the water stained with blood, the orcas left the scene. It was nothing new for them but an unforgettable experience for the watching birders.

I am amazed to witness such a change since I first went to Fair Isle in 1959, when grey seals had no real predators apart from man. Orcas have also hunted and been instrumental in reducing common seal numbers. By the end of the twentieth century, Scottish seals, both the grey and the common, had had to re-learn their relationship with the great black-and-white apex predator of the oceans. That's as it should be, and is how nature should work. It is unlikely that we will again see those big burgeoning populations of seals of the 1960s and '70s, when orcas had all but been removed from our waters. Maybe we didn't need an action plan, after all.

Elsewhere, orcas have reduced Steller's sea lions and sea otters off the northern coasts of the Pacific Ocean, and elephant seals and Minke whales in the Southern Ocean. Some believe this is due to the massive loss of great whales last century, when the young whales were the favoured food of orcas, forcing them to move down to smaller species. But what next? In May 2018, a group of people in an inflatable rib off the Moray coast found themselves surrounded by five orcas while a very frightened cow grey seal hid under their boat and even tried to climb on board. The orcas moved on, but while seeing orcas close up from sea kayaks must be very exciting, how long will it be before a very clever orca recognises that the people on board are edible? Or that divers are orca food encased in neoprene suits? Orcas, after all, are clever and learn to specialise. Perhaps, for the sake of our sea kayakers, there'll be another action plan along soon.

# Golden eagles – a new future?

A few years ago, the journal *British Birds* carried a media release on the results of the 2015 golden eagle survey, which highlighted a moderate increase in numbers as well as concern over continuing persecution in grouse moor regions. The latter is still really serious but there are other big issues with golden eagle conservation that are not being addressed.

One is that much of the uplands are severely degraded due to very long-term, and continuing, overgrazing by sheep and red deer, and excessive burning. In consequence, many eagle home ranges may have enough carrion to sustain the adults but inadequate live prey – small- to medium-sized mammals and birds – to successfully rear their young. This results in breeding success figures below 0.2 young per pair: one young being reared per five breeding pairs! There's also a high likelihood that those young that do fledge may be in poor condition due to food shortages while in their eyries. There is an urgent need for large-scale ecological restoration to restore scrub and woodland so as to increase levels of wildlife. This appalling state of affairs has been recognised for a century and recently brought into fresh focus through the discussions on rewilding.

It was also suggested that golden eagles had now reached 'favourable conservation status' in the UK. In my letter to the journal I commented, 'That is certainly not true for England, Wales and Northern Ireland, and even in Scotland this should also be judged on breeding success performance, not just the total population figure.' A frequent mistake, made even by eagle experts, is to assume that golden eagles are solely an upland species. The species has that distribution because of persecution and disturbance by humans for many centuries. Eagles in the north and west Highlands and in the Western Isles are now more regularly seen on land at sea level and close to houses because interference by crofters and shepherds has greatly reduced in the last few decades. Cultural breeding behaviour dictated by long-term persecution, especially in the eastern and southern heather moorlands, makes it difficult for them to spread onto lower, often more productive, ground in the east and south of Scotland.

Golden eagles can, and should, breed on low ground and in wooded landscapes, just like pairs I have watched elsewhere in Europe. In Sweden, I was shown the breeding site of a pair of golden eagles that was in a wooded valley amongst farmlands, forests and villages in the populated south of the country. It was a real eye-opener to me. In eastern Portugal, I saw a golden eagle eyrie on a wooded hillside of olive trees. The nest was not in a big tree and was less than 400 metres from the local road, yet the pair had raised three eaglets that year. We must think of golden eagles in a new way if we are to understand the pre-persecution range in Britain. In my own area of the eastern Highlands of Scotland, there are over twenty potential low-ground home ranges in Easter Ross, East Inverness and Moray that do not feature in the present historical baseline because of ancient extermination. Consequently, the present population may be less than half the potential in Scotland and the unused home ranges are often the ones with richer prey for eagles.

In recent memory, golden eagles have nested precariously in the Lake District and Northumberland's Kielder Forest, but both places have now lost their breeding pairs. It is important to look at England and Wales in a new light, bearing in mind Portugal and southern Sweden, for there are many potential nesting areas, from Devon and Hampshire northwards – including places such as the New Forest, Salisbury Plain and the Norfolk Brecks, where eagles could thrive as part of restored ecosystems. This will need pro-active translocations using young and immature eagles from Scotland, which can be carried out successfully, but which presently usually fail to come to fruition due to timidity.

Instead of spending all our time on preventing illegal persecution, why not have a bold triple approach for this iconic species, which also involves range recovery by translocation and rewilding the uplands to restore ecological productivity and live prey? What I find truly worrying for the future of nature is that there are people capable of reintroducing eagles to these places now, but such projects would attract opposition as well as demands for a massive science base, years of feasibility studies and stakeholder meetings and then, possibly, a small trial. In my letter to *British Birds*, I compared that approach to the recent and truly momentous decision for the UK to leave the European Union, carried out in a few months with no science and a paucity of rational facts.

# Winter

# Days in a real forest

In February 1995, I flew to Bucharest for my first visit to Romania and was collected from the airport by my friend Dr Christoph Promberger. I remember the excitement of driving over snowy roads to Braşov, hoping a wolf pack would dash across our path. That evening my mind was full of the talk of large predators, all of them no longer in my country. Christoph took me on to Zărneşti, where he had established a field station with Romanian biologists. He and his colleagues were studying wolves, bears and lynx in the Carpathian Mountains.

Next morning, we explored by skidoo a big valley in deep snow, checking and setting wolf traps as his team were eager to start radio tracking individual wolves. There were lots of prints: wolf, bear, wild boar, red deer and marten. In one place, the wolves had killed and eaten most of a roe deer and then dragged it under a bush for their night-time feeds. I saw a lot of birds, including black woodpecker, nutcrackers, thirty hawfinches and a three-toed woodpecker. The setting sun gave the snow-covered peaks of Piatra Craiului a rose-pink glow. I was very impressed.

One evening, we drove to meet Mosu, the local gamekeeper, and in the late afternoon walked with him to a hunter's tower. These wooden towers had been built by the State Forestry for bear hunting, although it hardly deserved that name when the bears were encouraged to come to feed on maize and fresh meat. The deposed president Nicolae Ceauşescu had been a fanatical hunter of bears in Communist times so bear numbers were artificially high due to supplementary feeding and protection. Great beech trees cast dark shadows across the snowy clearing in the forest. At just before six, two young brown bears walked in from the forest and squabbled over a feed of maize. To me, they looked huge, but my companion told me that they were only half-grown. He thought they were siblings and, by the way they behaved, he thought a big adult was nearby.

Mosu's beat was about 13,000 hectares of state forest, encompassing three valleys with steep, wooded sides, as well as a few small farms by the rivers. Six miles away, in a broad fertile valley, were towns and villages while Braşov, a city of 350,000 people, was only twenty miles distant. As we sat and watched the night creep in, we talked of nature. Christoph translated for Mosu and for me. Mosu knew exactly what was in his forest: there were 105 red deer, 120 roe deer, 160 to 180 wild boar and forty-three brown bears, as well as six lynx and two packs of wolves totalling five to seven animals. We had spent several days tracking some of them in the deep snow but had only seen two red deer and one bear in daytime.

Mosu was curious about Scotland and he found it difficult to believe that a similar sized area in the Scottish Highlands might hold 2,000 red deer and 400 roe deer. I said that we had killed all our bears, wolves, wild boar and lynx centuries ago and that all were extinct. I tried to explain about overgrazing by red deer and the lack of tree regeneration, but I'm not sure he understood because his woods showed excellent regeneration. With a big smile, he offered to come and reduce the deer for us. If he ever did, he would have been amazed by the difference in the size of our red deer, which are probably half the size of his. Finally, it was dark and we climbed down from our lair and drove off into the night.

For me, it was a chance to step back in time and explore a forest ecosystem in action. This was no special nature reserve: it was part of a state forest used for timber production, yet it contained many of the elements we prize so highly: natural regeneration aplenty, not only of timber trees but also of other trees and shrubs as well as flowering plants and berry bushes; forests of tall beeches were magnificent on the steep slopes and alder thickets overhung the crystal-clear rivers.

Even in winter, the ecological links were plain to see. Ravens croaked as we skidoo-ed forest trails tracking an elusive wolf pack. I often hear ravens at home in the hills and love their varied calls; if we could speak to ravens, we would learn a lot. It was clear from the evidence at a wolf-killed deer carcass that these clever birds knew the exact whereabouts of their local wolf pack. I'm sure that as soon as young ravens fly from their nests in wolf country, they learn from their parents that wolves are food providers. Ravens will never go hungry while the wolves remain.

On another day, after following the tracks of a lynx uphill, I turned into a beech wood and found the snow crust churned up by wild boar. They had been rooting for beech mast. The hard-packed snow was peppered with the brown litter of the forest floor, much to the benefit of a big flock of brambling searching for beechnuts. Without the activities of the wild boar, no beech mast would have been available for the small birds living in the forest. While leaning against a beech tree on a valley slope, I had great views of a middle spotted woodpecker working a dead tree.

Once again, I returned home with new thoughts about nature conservation. These visits to the wilder parts of the world always encouraged me to broaden my thinking about nature at home. I was then, and still am, distressed at the tree-less state of much of the Highlands, the degraded rivers and eroded hillsides. Yet at the same time I recognise the international value of many of our natural areas like the Cairngorms, the Caledonian forests and the Flow Country. They are not only very special, but are the bedrock of an incredible potential for ecological restoration.

# The deaf birder's bird

At dawn on a winter's day, it was snowing in the garden, and by the time I was ready to go for my morning walk, nearly an inch of snow lay on the ground. I love walking in fresh snow as it gives me a chance to find out what unseen creatures are around. When I reached the edge of a nearby plantation, I could see that a young roe deer had crossed my path only minutes before, leaving a trail of black slots. Further up the track were the distinctive prints of a brown hare, louping the road.

On my return there was nothing new except multiple tracks, etched in the snow, of a bird more usually obvious at dusk than at dawn – the common pheasant. The week before, my wife and I had walked this favourite route of ours just before sunset as dozens and dozens of pheasants were settling in the trees for their night-time roosts. The winter sun was setting in the south-west and the birds in the leafless birches were outlined against a golden sunset. As we walked by, some burst indignantly from the branches, others crowed loudly.

Nowadays, the 'deaf birder's bird', as Moira, calls them – knowing that I now find it hard to hear the high-pitched calls of small passerines – is the commonest bird in our immediate vicinity, as thousands of pheasants are reared and released for hunting. I could try closing my eyes and imagining that the sounds were in fact coming from great trees on beautiful mountain slopes in their native lands of Asia. That is something I would love to see, but I'm now too old to hike into the high Himalayas. I do remember, though, walking through dense woods in Japan with the acknowledged expert on the endemic copper pheasant. After three and a half hours of searching, we sat on a bench to eat our picnic. He pulled out a couple of his research papers and a quick read showed me that, on average, he had recorded a copper pheasant every four hours. After a twenty-minute break, we set off with fresh hope and, just minutes later, right on cue, a beautiful coppery-coloured bird, its trailing tail feathers seventy centimetres long, crossed our path and, like a ghost, disappeared into the dense undergrowth. Sometimes, sightings of new birds can be tantalisingly brief!

Pheasants are some of the most beautifully coloured birds in the world and the fifty or so species often live in stunning mountain and forest landscapes. The closest I came to seeing 'our' common pheasant in the wild was in western Mongolia, where they live in dense reed beds by montane lakes. Being good to eat, they were clearly shy of people and kept well-hidden when a group of locals from the university tried to show me one.

Back home in Scotland I find it bizarre that the commonest bird, and definitely the commonest by weight, in my backyard, as in many parts of Britain, is this introduced one. I also wonder why we just accept their continued presence, while we routinely endeavour to eradicate other alien species, and why it remains so difficult to get permission to reintroduce lost species.

# Giant pandas and thoughts of home

In December 2015, I had a most exciting week in Sichuan province, learning about giant pandas. Thanks to Iain Valentine, the then Director of the Giant Panda Project at Edinburgh Zoo, I was given a privileged visit to the research locations of his Chinese colleagues. They showed us their work and took us into some amazing places. This was my first visit to China so everything was new, exciting and different – Chengdu city has a population of 18 million, a far cry from my hometown of Forres in Moray.

I had a morning arrival after my flight from the UK and Iain had arranged to meet me at the hotel that evening. This gave me a chance to walk along the river near our hotel, where I saw plumbeous water redstarts, as well as the busyness of the city. I thought of the time about thirty years previously when my older daughter Rona lived here and spent some months teaching university students the principles of landscape remote sensing techniques. It was a different, older China then.

Next morning, Iain and I were driven to the city of Ya'an, to the southwest of Chengdu, and up into wooded hills to the Bifengxia Panda Base, where we saw the breeding pandas with their young, then the nursery unit with four baby pandas fast asleep in little wicker baskets. Outside this unit was the kindergarten area where the young ones lived when they were big enough to go outside. Further on were the enclosures where female pandas with larger young were kept; some of these would later be released into the wild.

The following day we drove north to the town of Duijangyan, for a brief visit to a panda research centre, before travelling on to the panda breeding centres at Wolong, in its impressive valley in the mountains of Sichuan. This was definitely the high point of my visit. The new panda HQ was a most impressive place built with funds from Hong Kong, its state-of-the-art layout tastefully constructed with local stone and landscaped with trees and bamboos. There were already eight groups of enclosures capable of holding thirty breeding females, as well as maternity units, laboratories, offices and an education centre. On two days we hiked to field stations in remote valleys, where teams of field staff carry out fieldwork and have built large electric-fenced enclosures as training sites for the gradual release of captive-bred pandas. It was great to see the teams, including graduates and professors, dedicated to field conservation, working with an ethos based on large ecosystems.

The Wolong Nature reserve itself covers 200,000 hectares, while the larger Sichuan panda ecosystem, at nearly a million hectares, is twice the size of the Cairngorms National Park. It contains seven giant panda reserves as well as other protected sites, and the aim is to improve connectivity throughout the whole ecosystem. The giant pandas are the flagship species but these mountains, rising from 1,200 to 6,250 metres, are a biodiversity hotspot: there are up to 6,000 species of plants, including magnolias, rhododendrons and bamboos, many of them endemic, making it the richest of any temperate region; 109 mammal species, including clouded and snow leopards, golden cat, golden monkey, red panda, takin and white-lipped deer; and more than 365 species of birds, 300 of them breeding, including Tibetan eared and white-eared pheasants.

There's more panda ecosystem in the next provinces to the north, and the latest estimate of giant pandas in the wild, based on field signs and DNA, is 1,864 individuals. Two thirds of them live in panda reserves belonging to the State Forestry of China. The aim is to restore damaged parts of the species range and increase their numbers; even now, with the lower total and the size of the available habitat, the population looks to be long-term secure. Looking out over this magnificent mountain range with its jagged snowy peaks and deep valleys of native forests and bamboos, I could see the importance of the giant panda, which is an icon of conservation. A strong worldwide partnership, led by China, is trying to protect this special mammal and its incredible ecosystem.

As ever when abroad, this time sitting on a rocky hillside in the backyard of the giant panda, I thought of nature conservation back home and it was very worrying. It's embarrassing to have to tell foreign colleagues that the vast majority of our native forests have gone. We have to do better and stop kidding ourselves that we are conservation leaders in the world. We must fast-track the restoration and conservation of large ecosystems to secure our nature, and our future. For me, that means ecosystem conservation taking precedence over economic activity in at least 40 per cent of our land and seas. Proactive work in the field must be aided by sound research, rather than held back. We need to be more entrepreneurial for nature, always aim high, recognise the importance of icons and remember to say 'when', not 'if'. On the world stage, it would, for example, be shocking if we continue to fail to restore the lynx to Scotland.

# Bounty from the seas

It was a frosty morning in March 498 A.D. and the two boys' foot-steps did not break through the soft sand along the tideline of Culbin Bar in Moray. They had been searching for dead birds or fish washed in on the tide, but their pickings were poor. As they turned the corner of the last great dune, clothed in marram grass, they could hear a commotion of splashing in the gut and then saw a huge whale thrashing in the water. They had never seen this before but had heard tales from their grandfathers, so they rushed homewards over the dunes, bursting with the excitement of their discovery.

End of winter was a difficult time for the folk eking a living on the Moray coast. They were down to their last supplies so any chance of extra food was important. In no time the elders had gathered everyone together, while some of the women set off to tell nearby villages of the discovery. The men found the whale still in the channel of the gut but there was no way it could escape on an ebbing tide. To make sure, some men waded into the water to plunge sharp spears into its heart and head. Weighing nearly forty tonnes, this male sperm whale was going to provide a massive boost to the people living in this part of Moray and would prove to be the difference between starvation and survival.

Once the whale was dead, the men started to hack out big chunks of blubber and meat but were dwarfed by the massive mammal wallowing in the bloody water. The last time this group of people had harvested a whale on the shore was forty years or more before and the old men remembered the incredible supply of meat and blubber, as well as the bones and the huge reservoir of fine oil in the head. For early man, beached whales were a bonanza from the seas. Wildlife also benefitted – during the days, the whale carcass was thronged by birds like gulls, white-tailed eagles, ravens and crows, and even snow buntings joined in to eat tiny scraps of fat. At night, wolves, bears, foxes and badgers scavenged the carcass. It was suddenly a time of plenty for humans and wildlife, and it was an example of recycling the biological productivity of the oceans back on to the land. Usually the process is the reverse as rivers take nutrients and biological matter out to sea so this represented a perfect circle in nature.

Now what do we, modern humans, do? First, we try to get the whales back into the sea, often unsuccessfully. Then the whale rapidly turns into a problem – whose problem? Why did the whale die and how do we dispose of it? And, before long, it is dragged away to be buried in a landfill site. What an incredible waste of life that is. Could we not salvage and use the 1,500 litres of amazing oil? Could we use the meat and bones for garden fertiliser? And with some of these monsters, in remoter spots, why can we not leave the carcasses on the beach for mammal, bird and insect scavengers? For many years after, we could marvel at the size of the bones of a sperm whale.

When I first wandered the Nairn and Culbin Bars, on the coast of the Moray Firth in the 1960s, there were lots of cetacean vertebrae on the shingle. I enjoyed looking at them, holding them and leaving them there, after marvelling at the lichens growing on these great relics. But slowly people carted them off as souvenirs and none now remain. It is now illegal, in fact, to remove whale and dolphin parts, but I don't think most people know that. The advice should always be leave it so that others, especially young people, exploring our coasts can have the same enjoyment as we did when we were young.

I think we need to seek a new relationship with whales now that we have stopped killing them. Their populations are increasing and it's likely we will see more strandings. Beached whales could be a natural phenomenon rather than always being the malign results of human activities. Every time whales strand we, nowadays, look for a human cause, but are we correct to do so? In January 2016, twenty-nine sperm whales died on the coasts of the North Sea. They were all young males and I wondered why that was. Could it be that there are sufficient mature bulls with the breeding herds of female sperm whales further south in the Atlantic and that intense competition is pushing the young males into dangerous places? Whale music carrying through the oceans may not always be benign – sometimes it's a warning to other whales, reminding them to stay away.

Although losses are tragic, they are not likely to influence the fecundity of the population as a whole. After all, through the millennia, this has simply been a natural way of recycling the bounty of the seas.

# Genes and wildlife management

At the end of the nineteenth century, the red squirrel was all but extinct in northern Scotland, with maybe a few remaining in Abernethy Forest. In 1844, Lady Lovat imported and released red squirrels at Beauly near Inverness and they exploded into the countryside – by the early twentieth century they had colonised most of the Scottish Highlands. They fared so well, in fact, that they became a concern to many foresters caring for their trees.

During the Second World War, many of the mature pinewoods of Scotland were cut down for the war effort and it was not until the 1960s that replanting really got under way. In consequence, the squirrels started to disappear in the outlying areas through the loss of cone-bearing old trees and this was almost certainly exacerbated when pine martens started to increase in Wester Ross and break out of their refugia. The newly planted pine plantations were supplying a rich prey base of voles and respite from persecution for the martens, allowing them to rapidly increase after a century of intense killing. By the 1970s, red squirrel distribution had contracted and at the turn of the century the limits were near Tain and Garve, and were contracting further still.

In 2008, a highly successful translocation project saw forty-three red squirrels moved from Moray and Strathspey to Dundonnell in Wester Ross, and the population boomed (see *A good day with red squirrels*). What fascinated me was why these ones were breeding so fast and yet the ones on the edge of the range, also with nearby available habitat, were not.

It seemed too soon to suggest that it was due to my stirring up the genes and I didn't get much support for that argument, nor for my other suggestion that low numbers of squirrels at the edge of the northern range were too closely related and behaving like siblings. The Dundonnell ones, I argued, must have woken up on the first morning and suddenly met all these squirrels that they had never met before. Was that an explanation for the boom in numbers? It struck me as a bit like village teenagers finding girlfriends or boyfriends in villages other than their own.

In 2007, on a fact-finding trip to Switzerland I learnt more about lynx from my friends, Urs and Christianne Breitenmoser, world experts on the species. One evening a group of us were in a restaurant, when Urs received a phone call. One of the live traps had just caught a lynx. There followed a mad exodus and a fast drive and we found ourselves in a Jura forest in the pitch black. There, by torchlight, was the lynx. It was later translocated to the Alps from the Jura, part of a planned gene exchange between the two sub-populations. The scientists wanted to be sure that there were no problems with the genetics of the new Swiss population.

It was another field experience that suggested to me that wildlife managers would need to think about these things more often in the future. I was with my friend Tim Appleton, the manager of the Rutland Water Nature Reserve. We had walked over marshland to one of the release cages for the osprey translocation project in 1996. It was a sunny day and I nearly stepped on a grass snake, the first that I'd seen for many years, and then another couple of them sunbathing. I thought they were beautiful and I asked Tim where the next grass snakes might be, considering that his land was surrounded by intensive agriculture. He replied that they'd probably be in the next nature reserve. I was shocked but now that's how it is with many species of wildlife when natural areas, on the low ground, are like gems dotted through a landscape of agriculture. It would be great to have corridors, but I guess we'll just have to be clever at moving and swapping individuals between locations to maintain genetic health. Essential job creation on an epic scale.

# The true worth of nature

In recent years I've started to hear the call by some conservationists that the only way we will protect nature is by giving everything a monetary value. Immediately I think of Oscar Wilde's description of a cynic as a person who 'knows the price of everything and the value of nothing'. I was fortunate to be starting my life in nature conservation when we had inspirational leaders like Peter Scott, Max Nicholson and George Waterston. The ethos that I grew up with was that humans, as the most dominant species on Earth, had a clear duty to protect and conserve the natural world and its incredible array of species.

Of course, that was in the era when duty was valued very highly; older people, both women and men, had come through the Second World War, where duty was second nature. Sadly, in recent decades, duty and care within society seems often to have given way to putting the individual first. I remember a Scottish Natural Heritage director once saying that, in the future, wildlife had to be useful to us if it was to be protected. I was appalled, as it promoted the view that humans were all-important. It was part of the argument that nature should have a price. If costed as 'natural capital', it was more likely to be protected. What an awful view.

I shudder at the idea of a world where we have to judge whether we keep a place for nature – say, a wood or marsh – by how much its constituent parts are worth compared to its value if we developed it for housing or industry. It's just crackers.

What I do agree with is a need for all individuals to understand how the lives and welfare of themselves, their children and their grandchildren depend on the living Earth's ecosystems: that the oxygen we breathe is created through photosynthesis taking place in trees, plants and plankton; that the water we drink comes from rain falling; the food we eat grows in soils created over millennia; and the sun provides us with light and heat, although sometimes too much in some places.

Fortunately, people are taking note. They are being more caring of nature and there is an increasing mood that something has to be done. I hope it does not take too long, for time is short to save our planet Earth for all creatures, and for us.

# New Year birding

I went out birding on the first day of 2017, trying for a New Year's Day list but knowing that I would never again see 100 species on 1st January in the north of Scotland, as I did in 1975. Despite a surprisingly long period of mild weather, there was a strong, cold, northerly wind blowing on to the Moray coast. There were big waves breaking over the harbour walls, so it was not surprising that when I looked out from the headland at Burghead, I didn't manage to see any scoters or red-throated divers in the rough swell. For a 'big bird day' the weather was against me, I did not start at dawn, I stopped to first-foot friends and I'm not as good a birder now as then, especially at hearing small birds. My last one at dusk was a woodcock, giving me a total of sixty-four species.

A lingering flock of forty-eight waxwings in Forres, and eight bramblings feeding under the beech trees near Elgin were nice finds. But the most poignant was the covey of five grey partridges just inland from Findhorn Bay. They could be the last here of what was a common bird in the 1970s. And once those five die, they will all be gone. There are so many species that were easy to see back then but have disappeared or become rare now. Of course, there are a few others that have become so much more common, like pink-footed geese, and those that we have restored to Scotland, such as the red kite. But the general trend in species and abundance is downwards and it's a stark reminder of the huge task we have in restoring nature.

My wife often pulls my leg by saying, 'I guess you like that person because he agrees with you.' Don't we all? But the real find is someone with an even more ambitious vision. I have already mentioned Professor Edward Wilson's book *Half-Earth*, which argues that we need to dedicate half the surface of the Earth to nature. But it bears repeating as it's such a convincing argument and concurs with my long-held view that nature conservation needs now to be about restoring and conserving very large functioning ecosystems – and I mean very, very large – within which the conservation of individual species is achieved and the Earth's life processes are maintained. Even in Britain this is a mammoth – but essential – task.

All of us who enjoy, use or work with nature must stand up and fight for it, because at the moment the conservation of the natural world is woefully inadequate, despite sterling efforts by many people and organisations. Raise the issue politically, socially and economically. Demand a real change. We owe it to future generations, so that they will live on a good Earth. Why not give a copy of *Half-Earth* to your MP, or, in Scotland or Wales, your MSP or AM? And add a note saying you want to meet them, once they have read it, to find out what they intend to do. As Humboldt said, 150 or so years ago, 'The most dangerous worldview is the worldview of those who have not viewed the world.'

# White stoat, green grass

Back in February 2017, a most beautiful ermine (white stoat) visited our garden several times. Talk about a sore thumb: the poor stoat was glaringly obvious in a landscape lacking snow. Winters with snow cover from November to mid-March, when ermine were in their element, seem to be a thing of the past. In 2017, the grass was growing long enough to harvest for my eight-year-old daughter's guinea pigs – not surprisingly, since there had been a series of beautiful sunny days since the New Year. It had been better, in fact, than the summer before.

I'd been trying to photograph the stoat and finally managed it. It was only a long-distance shot because just when I thought I'd got a close photo, a wood lorry sent it scuttling over the bank. Later that month, I also saw a weasel darting across the garden. Perhaps I was seeing this special garden wildlife simply because I'd been spending more time gazing out the window as I rested after an operation. It had also given me a chance to read and think.

One thing that had caught my mind in the papers was a forward look, by a Microsoft think tank, at the jobs our children will be doing in ten years' time. One of the ten 'new jobs' was 'Rewilding Strategist'. It was good to see the need for ecosystem recovery becoming mainstream, but surely we should be getting on with it rather than waiting? And some of us could say, 'Well, isn't that what we are doing now?' But then maybe it's because we don't call ourselves a 'strategist'. I'd better redo my CV.

One book I really enjoyed was Dimitra Papagianni and Michael Morse's *The Neanderthals Rediscovered*. Although in my work of restoring species and ecosystems, the problems are usually to do with modern human exploitation and damage, I've always been fascinated by our original role within natural ecosystems. For most of our history on Earth, we've just been a very efficient apex predator in nature; the tipping point to becoming over-dominant is relatively recent. So can we – and should we – try to emulate our original role?

I read an article in the *Guardian* magazine about the 'wolf problem' in Finland and the arguments about how many wolves there should be. Some say there are far too many, others say they have a right to be there and that we should leave them alone. But it's incorrect to think that 20,000 years ago we 'left them alone'. The difference is that when numbers were high we threw spears and rocks at them, and hunted their young for furs, and when numbers were low it was not worth the effort. There was a sort of natural system, unlike the recent millennium with metal traps, poisons and high-powered rifles.

It's very encouraging that conservation and legal protection can restore species, even the big predators in Europe, but what happens if our efforts are so successful that they may cause threats to other species or rural people? The 'Rewilding Strategist' is going to have to learn how to regulate species that boom in present-day conditions to the detriment of others. In northern Scotland, the middle-guild predators – fox, badger, marten and otter – are thriving under societal changes and/or legal protection and, in the absence of the top predators like lynx, wolf and bear, there are few natural checks on numbers (see 'Too many badgers'). As a great supporter of restoring species, I can see the dilemmas ahead. I want to see beavers restored over much larger areas and the lynx brought back home, but I also recognise the need for robust management. To me, the conservation of the species, as a whole, in as big a range as possible is more important that the conservation of the individual of the species. We are in interesting and challenging times, but the important thrust is to massively increase the areas of natural ecosystems.

# Always remember the bigger picture

In recent years, I've started cataloguing over sixty years' worth of field notebooks, diaries, lectures, papers and reports with the intention, and hope, of writing books ... such as this one! It's very time-consuming and made more so by coming across fascinating letters and wildlife records that side-track me into memories.

I'm surprised how often wildcat comes up, either seen alive or hanging dead from a fence. In the 1960s and 1970s they were pretty widespread, whereas the other mid-sized carnivores were surprisingly uncommon. Between 1960 and 1963, as a full-time field ornithologist in the Scottish Highlands, I failed to see a pine marten despite searching for them. Badgers were scarce and I well remember an old crofter on the Black Isle telling me that a fox he killed there in 1952 was the first seen for nearly a century. That's nearly unbelievable now.

I'm a great believer that history is an important part of successful wildlife management and it is essential to take it into account when thinking about ecological restoration, nowadays called rewilding. It's clear now that hybridisation with feral domestic cats, and disease transfer, have been at the root of the recent problems of the decline of the wildcat, but what of the other problems? What is the bigger picture? It is very difficult to remember exactly what one saw fifty years ago but I'm sure I remember that the wildcats I saw, either alive or dead, all looked like wildcats rather than hybrid feral cats. Could it be the case that when wildcats were common there was far less chance of them breeding with feral cats? In fact, I might suggest that they probably killed any feral cat they found in the wrong place. And there was no shortage of domestic cats around farms and crofts then because rodents were common when grain was stored on farm.

Clearly, killing by trap, snare, poison or gun reduced numbers in those days but somehow that persecution seemed to have had a greater impact on the other middle-guild predatory mammals than on wildcats. This almost certainly changed later in the century when spotlights became effective ways of shooting predators at night. Nowadays, badger, fox, pine marten and even otter are probably commoner than they have ever been in northern Scotland, yet wildcat is in serious decline. Could there be a link? Could the high numbers of its dog-like competitors put the wildcat at a disadvantage? I have a sneaking suspicion that could be the case.

With that thought, I think it's necessary to look at the bigger picture: not to concentrate solely on the individual species but to think of the species' place in larger ecosystems. We also need to recognise that successful restoration of iconic species may be very difficult unless we think and act in a more holistic way. This brings me back to the debate about lynx.

When I hear people say that we cannot bring back the lynx as that would really put paid to the wildcat, I wonder if they really understand the functioning of ecosystems for wildlife conservation. I remember one winter riding a horse through deep snow in a Carpathian forest and coming across a wildcat eating the remains of a roe deer under a hazel tree. Earlier, I had followed the track of a lynx along the forest track for maybe two kilometres. My hosts, experts on large carnivores, knew exactly where I had seen the wildcat because they had seen it with its kill in the snow several days earlier. To them, lynx and wildcat were both part of the wildlife community in the mountains of Romania.

The return of the lynx to Scotland is truly an essential part of restoring nature to our country and re-establishing a functioning ecosystem to show the real benefits of rewilding. Instead of being a threat to wildcat, the impacts of lynx on fox and badger would undoubtedly, in my view, benefit the wildcat by reducing the numbers and ranging behaviour of its competitors.

For successful wildlife management, especially in the field of ecological restoration, we must have bold and broad visions. I encourage the team charged with saving the wildcat always to remain innovative, prepared to change, determined to try all avenues and never give up, and to increase their expertise in true fieldwork. That will be difficult in an era of over-cautious science and risk-averse bureaucracy, which can, so often, lead to inactivity and delay.

# The assassin of the night

I saw my first eagle owl in 1972 in the limestone hills of southern France when leading a group of birdwatchers. We watched the male roosting on a white cliff and our local guide said its mate had young in a small cave. In later years, I saw another roosting in a rocky gorge in Mongolia, and every now and then I would see one on my travels, for they occur throughout much of Europe, Asia and North Africa. One time I visited a trout farm in northern Sweden and the owner told me of an eagle owl that came at night in winter, when very hungry, to scoop out the occasional trout. That reminded me of watching the even bigger Blakiston's fish owls hunting in the warm volcanic streams flowing through the snowy landscape of Hokkaido. It was a Finnish friend who told me they called eagle owls the 'assassin of the night' because of their size, power and silent but deadly hunting.

In Britain, I sometimes saw tame eagle owls at falconry centres and wildlife parks, as they are easy birds to keep and breed. The public find them exciting, for they are stunning birds, weighing up to four kilograms, standing sixty-five centimetres tall and with a wingspan of up to two metres. They have large, staring orange eyes and big ear tufts. My experience of the eagle owl, then, was of a tame bird sitting on a block in a garden or perched on a falconer's arm. In the 1970s and early 1980s, one of my tasks with the RSPB was to combat the illegal taking of peregrines and other raptors from the wild for falconry. These incidents often involved people who also kept eagle owls, so professionally we came to regard them as tame birds rather than a wild species. They are also quite skilled at escaping from captivity and living in the wild.

I had a chance to change my mind in 1985 when I was privileged to watch a pair of eagle owls nesting in a quarry in Moray. The female laid four white eggs in an earthy hollow under a cliff-face juniper bush. Only one of the eggs hatched; normally there would be two to four young in a brood. My assistant Colin Crooke and I decided to ring the young owl, and I vividly remember the blend of excitement and concern as the female threatened us with outspread wings and clacking bill just four metres away on the nest ledge. Colin kept a close eye on her and I quickly caught her young. In the past, I had been mobbed by nesting tawny owls but this was really scary. We put the chick back and slithered down the slope.

Very sadly, her mate was killed that autumn on the public road. He'd made a mistake when eating a road-killed rabbit and was killed by a car himself. We never heard of the ringed youngster but the female lived another nine years laying infertile eggs. We thought about finding her a new mate, but in those days I regarded them as escapees or released birds. There was no proof of their origin, no rings, no jesses to show they were from captivity, but just an assumption (and maybe prejudice) that they were not wild.

In 2004, the BBC producer Fergus Beeley asked me to present a television documentary on eagle owls and it turned out to be a fascinating and fraught story. We started on a January dawn at a nest site monitored by Major Tony Crease, the Ministry of Defence conservation officer in North Britain. Suddenly there was an eerily deep 'oo-hu', immediately answered in an echoing duet. It was Britain's only known breeding eagle owls at their secret nest site in northern England. As the sun came up they fell silent, but the ghostly calls are vivid in my memory. Tony had followed their fortunes and given them security since 1996. In that time, the pair had reared twenty young in their hidden valley, but none of the ringed birds had been reported until one of the 2003 young was found dead, electrocuted under a transmission pole on a Shropshire farm, about 200 kilometres south of its nest. Sadly, one of the adult owls was later killed.

In this country, the eagle owl is an enigma. Should these great owls be here in Britain or not? Are they British? Do they belong here? Were they once a native breeding species? Will they be here again? These are contentious questions. A review of about ninety records by the British Ornithologists' Union dismissed the eagle owl's claim to be British, at least within the last 200 years, and many conservationists are against them because they might kill protected birds. Undoubtedly, the eagle owls seen in the wild in Britain in the last fifty years have all (or nearly all) escaped from captivity or been released.

With the film crew, I visited southern Sweden in September 2004 and witnessed the release of young eagle owls as part of the Swedish project 'Berguv', their name for eagle owl. Sweden's eagle owls suffered a dramatic decline last century, mainly due to persecution by hunters and farmers, but a countrywide series of conservation projects, including releases, and protection, had restored them. The situation was similar in Germany and from there they recolonised Belgium and the Netherlands.

In Switzerland, where numbers rose last century from nearly extinct to 120 pairs, I visited Adrian Aebischer to learn about the wanderings of the young. A commonly held view in Britain is that eagle owls do not move far from their nest sites. His research, using radio telemetry, showed that some young had travelled as much as 320 kilometres through the Alps, even over 3,000-metre mountain passes. Some Scandinavian birds had flown nearly twice that distance. And as populations grow, young birds need to move to find new locations. So not all eagle owls are stay-at-homes.

On our travels in mainland Europe, I was struck by the fact that eagle owls were not necessarily owls of wild places, as is commonly thought, but are quite happy around towns, villages and industrial sites. There they can often find more prey in the form of rabbits, rats, crows or hedgehogs than in remote forests. So there was another myth exploded – the fact that an eagle owl might perch on a roof is no proof that it's tame. Eagle owls have been seen in towns, villages and built-up areas in the UK, and such behaviour has been used to prove they were not wild.

Eagle owls are very capable hunters and will eat most things smaller than themselves. At the English nest, the favourite food was rabbit, which was plentiful at the time. They will kill a whole range of birds and mammals, and even insects, amphibians and fish. They are principally ambush hunters at twilight or night, swooping on unsuspecting moving prey. They learn to deal with difficult prey; for example, they tear off the prickles before eating hedgehogs.

In the Netherlands, the researcher Paul Voskamp showed me a buzzard that had been killed and eaten the previous night. They even kill peregrine falcons and, on rare occasions, ospreys in Sweden and Finland. These are caught as they roost at night in trees or on their nests. I was heartened that, while holding the remains of a buzzard, Paul regarded this as part of the ecosystem – one raptor killing another. That's my view as well; it is a fact of life in nature. When adult, the eagle owls themselves have no predators except man, but the nestlings can be killed by foxes and badgers.

Looking back into the history of eagle owls in Britain, it's difficult to find evidence of breeding. There are a few reports of remains at excavations of archaeological sites, with one person even identifying eagle owl pellets. But it's important to remember that absence of evidence is not evidence of absence. Interestingly, they were often in the north and east, suggestive of immigrants. In my view it's now impossible to say that none were vagrants from mainland Europe, and when they were common on mainland Europe, vagrancy was likely. The interesting question is whether or not they could return, now that the eagle owl has increased and spread in mainland Europe after long centuries of persecution.

So what do I think now? Firstly, it seems to me inconceivable that eagle owls did not reach Britain after the last Ice Age: they are a widespread and adaptable species; they are not averse to crossing water; they live on islands off the Norwegian coast where they hunt seabirds. I do think they were wiped out as a breeding bird in Britain long ago, probably half a millennium ago. But why? It's probably those eerie night-time calls that make the hairs on the back of your neck stand up. Humans throughout the world regarded owls as spooky birds, often harbingers of death or bad luck. Even now owls are killed in some parts of the world because of those legends. Eagle owls would have been particularly easy to kill. They make a lot of noise so were easy to locate, and their nests were often easily accessible on the ground or at the bottom of cliffs. And they defend their nests from humans, making them easy to kill with stones, sticks or spears and, later, guns.

And what of the future? The recent increases in mainland Europe, including just across the sea in Belgium and the Netherlands, make it near enough certain that some will cross to Britain, and possibly have already done so. Once here under their own steam, they will of course be a British bird (again?) and will probably be afforded legal protection, as elsewhere in Europe.

They are big, exciting birds and will be a key species in the countryside. They will be difficult neighbours for some species, but if we are true to the principles of nature conservation we cannot protect just the species we like. It cannot be right to say we would welcome eagle owls if they ate only rats and crows, and not if they preyed on peregrines or corncrakes. In fact, they might impact some of the species that are expanding and causing problems for other species, such as pine martens, young badgers or goshawks. In nature, as in so many things, we have to accept the rough with the smooth.

# Is the common mole a soil canary?

Most gardeners and most farmers don't like molehills, but how many recognise the value of the mole? Late winter 2015 was mild in northern Scotland and was boom time for busy moles in my part of the world. But it was where the moles were burrowing that I found so interesting and disturbing.

Why did I see more molehills in the narrow verges of the main road from Forres to Elgin than I did in most of the rich farm fields of the Moray plain? Most of these deep, fertile soils were used intensively for growing cereals with some break crops, but the days of mixed agriculture, using cattle dung in rotations, were mostly gone. The spring barley was being planted and the fields would soon flush that beautiful fresh green, but rarely would a molehill be seen. How different things were just inland, where I lived, among the upland stock-rearing farms.

Across the road from our cottage stands one of the neighbouring farmer's dung heaps and every spring he is out spreading manure over his grass fields, later to be cut for silage. Moles are more obvious in these fields, which are regularly foraged for invertebrates by starlings and winter thrushes. Further up in the glens, I see that the permanent pastures are chequered with molehills and I know that moles range high in the hills in the pockets of good soils.

So where have the moles gone on the low ground? It's not so long ago that mole catchers were in great demand and, despite their best efforts with traps and poisons, the moles were never defeated. Is it deep ploughing that kills off moles? I think that is certainly part of the change. Or is it the intensive and continual use of artificial fertilisers and crop chemicals, in the absence of cattle dung rotations, which has killed off the soil invertebrates?

Maybe both. The absence of moles in intensively farmed fields will be a result of an absence of worms, their essential food, as well as losing out to deep ploughing.

I remember how annoying molehills were when I used to cut hay for my cattle and sheep, using an old bar mower, and I'd hear the clatter of a mole-turned stone denting the blade. Despite that, I always remembered that worms and moles were an essential part of 'keeping the land in good heart'. Charles Darwin called earthworms 'nature's ploughs'. The activities of worms enhance the fertility and health of soils; they work away at moving and decomposing plant material, aerating and stabilising soils, releasing nutrients, promoting plant growth and sequestering carbon. Goodness, they pay their way. And the moles also create tunnels that help aerate the soils and allow water penetration, as well as being voracious feeders on invertebrates harmful to plants.

Information on moles in the UK is surprisingly scant. What is the scale of the decline of moles, and worms, due to intensive agriculture in, say, the last fifty years? I can find figures of a million worms per hectare in naturally fertile soils, but what are the densities nowadays in fields of intensive cereals? I believe the loss must be truly massive. I remember the fields once hosting birds searching for invertebrates, blizzards of black-headed gulls following the plough and buzzards shuffling over winter cereal fields eating worms, where now I see none or very few. I would like to know the scale of this decline and its effects on long-term soil health. Might it be as alarming for humans in the long term, as it is now to earthworms and moles? It's probable that the scarcity of moles is an indicator of collapsing soil ecosystems, on top of soil erosion and compaction. If so, there's no doubt the mole is a 'canary' for the health of our soils. This issue is too serious to ignore. There's a critical need for strong land ethics and a dramatic change in farming practices.

# Why mentors matter

Every now and then I receive an email, a letter drops into my letterbox or I meet someone from long ago, and they remind me of a time and place special to them. Typically, the message might say something like, 'I always remember you taking me down the cliffs of Fair Isle to ring storm petrels in 1966. It sparked my lifetime interest in nature,' or 'do you remember you showed me that eagle's nest?' It is always nice to think you've helped people to have a more interesting life by knowing or being involved in nature, and even more so when you helped that person decide to have a career in wildlife. I know from experience that mentors have the power to shape lives.

My mum and dad were my first mentors; they encouraged me to run wild in the local woods and fields, to learn to make dens, catapults, bows and arrows, and to start taking a deep interest in the natural world. My mother told me the names of flowers and accepted the constant arrival of feathers, bird skulls and, in spring, a glass jar of frogspawn. They encouraged me to keep a notebook and to be careful with nature during our explorations, usually brought to a daily end by my mum calling to the woods in the late evening: 'Come in and get washed for school in the morning!' The other mums were doing the same.

In my teens, I had several important birding mentors. Firstly, my Scoutmaster John Everett encouraged my enthusiasm for birds and wildlife, and took our troop of scouts to camp in exciting places such as the New Forest or the Dorset or Cornish coasts, great for wildlife. One of our favourite camping sites was Crackington Haven, from where we could hike out to a headland, the Cambeak, to watch bird migration and the daily flights of local seabirds. John had a copy of the *Handbook of British Birds*, the ornithological bible at that time, and whenever I saw a new species I was able to read up on it. The next day you could have tested me – I would have taken in every word.

I started my nature diaries and I soon met others involved with birdwatching in southern Hampshire. Old Dr Suffern at Titchfield Haven helped many young birdwatchers to hone their bird identification skills on weekend walks through the marshes. Pedalling my bike as fast as possible from home to the haven always brought a feeling that we might see something special to add to my notebook. I remember one very cold February day counting thirty-two beautiful smew, a rare duck for us, flighting into the haven.

I then started to go birding at Farlington Marshes and my chance to learn from that very special Portsmouth Group of the 1950s (including David Billett, Taff Rees and Eddie Wiseman) was paved by my finding a rare aquatic warbler in a ditch on the marsh. Walking back with me to the site, I bet they were wondering if a kid like me could really identify an aquatic warbler. But there it was! I had won my spurs and was accepted by what was probably the most talented group of birdwatchers at field identification in Britain in that era. I learnt so much from them about the long-distance identification of waders, wildfowl and other birds in Langstone Harbour.

Peter Davis, the warden at Fair Isle Bird Observatory, was a great teacher when I went there as his young assistant in 1959. It was there that I really learned the trade of bird ringing and identifying migrant birds as well as ringing and studying the great seabird colonies of the island. Peter also recommended me to take over from him when he retired from the observatory wardenship four years later.

And Fair Isle was where I met one of the most influential mentors of my life: George Waterston from Edinburgh, who arrived at the Observatory, his very special love, in September 1959. I came under his spell. He gave me great encouragement and the following spring I went to work for him for four years as a RSPB warden with Operation Osprey at Loch Garten. While there, Dick and Marian Fursman were a great inspiration to me. I was Dick's assistant for four summers. He was a recently retired RAF Wing Commander and had a natural ability to encourage and teach me many of life's skills. Many of the older field naturalists in the RSPB, The Nature Conservancy and the Scottish Ornithologists' Club also encouraged and guided me in those early years in Scotland, such exciting times for a young birder.

But it was George who was always urging me to really understand the ospreys and to check out reports of rare breeding birds, and he introduced me to a whole range of very interesting people in the Scottish Highlands. For many years, 21 Regent Terrace, where he and Irene lived and had their offices, was like a second home to me, with great craíc over a glass of malt whisky, the chance to meet ornithologists from around the world and the constant planning of new things we should do. George imbued in me a bold attitude towards new projects, telling me that if you start five, one will go brilliantly, three will work well and one might fail, but don't let that put you off. Learn from the pitfalls but concentrate on the successful ones. It was wise advice and I found it very sad that he should die too soon without knowing how brilliantly projects like Operation Osprey and the return of the sea eagles turned out. I'm now Honorary President of the Fair Isle Observatory Trust and 2019 was my 60th year of knowing and loving that special island. I'm sure George would be pleased to know that I helped carry his baton, over all these years, for the island he loved.

# Ecological resilience
## for our grandchildren's grandchildren

If you were to compare much of the Scottish countryside with a house, it would have missing slates, broken windows and peeling paint and the front door would stand ajar. The renovation of an old building is one way to build our personal future. Our family, our house, our health, our security and our work are essential to our wellbeing, but the ecosystem in which we live is generally uncared for and unloved.

Over many centuries, we have laid a heavy hand on our land and seas. Scotland has seen woodland cover stripped away, open range overgrazed and burnt, rivers degraded, soils over-exploited, chemical onslaughts, pollution, over-use of fish stocks and an ever-increasing loss of biodiversity.

Like many countries, Scotland has now recognised the potential dangers of climate breakdown and we have set encouragingly high targets to increase the use of renewable energy, a tribute to our government in Edinburgh and our people. Scotland is making headway there and with many other issues, including recycling, reducing pollution and cleaning up pit bings and industrial dereliction. But, so far, we have not tackled in a similarly large way the health of the ecosystems essential for life in future centuries.

Just like renovating an abandoned building, we must now repair the environment and ensure that the life processes of our land and seas are working effectively. For our descendants, the impacts of climate breakdown, biodiversity collapse, burgeoning human populations and other environmental problems of the future will have a higher chance of being ameliorated if we restore the Earth's ecosystems to good health.

We have no choice, if we think of those descendants, but to start a major programme of ecological restoration. All degraded open land must be regenerated, most of it re-wooded to benefit carbon capture, oxygen production, watershed management, climate impacts and biodiversity gains. Our seas, oceans and marine life need special care that will require a major increase in non-fished protected areas. Our farmers must recognise and address the problems of over-used farmland, of chemical contamination and loss of soil structures and biodiversity.

If you google land use, ecosystems, climate change, land reform and similar issues, you find an impressive array of reports, strategies and promises for Scotland. Too often these reinforce the dominance of present day use by us now; for example, Scotland's Land Use Strategy was headed, 'Getting the best from our land'. Should it not be, 'Giving the best to our land'? Maybe that's why there is such concern, by some, about long-term ecological security and why there are few examples of major progress on the ground. Is the uncomfortable truth that those who should be shouting from the rooftops don't wish it to be known what is happening on their watch?

So what do we need to do in Scotland, and across the UK as a whole? Parliament must take the lead. It should establish a new type of Land Ethics Commission made up of bold, far-seeing people to examine how to ensure a more secure ecological future for our descendants. A national land ethics plan must then encourage essential changes through a carrot and stick approach. All landowners and users should audit their impact on the environment, just as we are required to do if we build a house. No longer will it be fair to society, as a whole, to say, 'My family has worked the land this way for centuries.' For example, maintaining extensive areas of degraded open land for deer stalking, grouse shooting or low-density sheep rearing puts our future in jeopardy.

It's going to be a tough call but we have no option if we want our grandchildren's grandchildren to inherit a healthy country. Leading thinkers suggest that half the Earth's lands and seas need to be managed for nature and natural processes if the planet is to provide us with a sustaining future. They are right. That's the uncomfortable truth.

# Author's note

Four of the essays in this collection are based on documents or articles that were written or published previously, as below:

Rewilding – ecological restoration (**page 23**): *This is based on my foreword to the Bird Fair prospectus, 13th May 2016.*

Selective land management in Abernethy Forest (**page 42**): *I based this on a letter I wrote to the Cairngorms National Park on 4th December 2013.*

Traditional cattle and biodiversity (**page 60**): *This is drawn from my February 1998 document, 'The importance of traditional cattle for woodland biodiversity in the Scottish Highlands'.*

Thoughts on wild red grouse (**page 78**): *This essay is based on my letter of November 2012 to Scottish Natural Heritage.*

Roy Dennis MBE has unparalled expertise as a field naturalist, having worked in conservation, rare species tracking and species reintroductions, as well as directing projects for the RSPB and other organisations. As a broadcaster and educator, he has made documentaries and been a regular presenter on the BBC's *Autumnwatch* and *Springwatch,* as well as other programmes. His Wildlife Foundation of 25 years' standing is internationally recognised for its work in conservation and wildlife protection.